The Christmas Blitz, 1940.

MANCHESTER FIRE BRIGADE

above: Steamer and crew (believed Upton Street). *opposite:* Twenty pumps were needed to fight the blaze at Jewsbury & Brown, Ardwick Green, 21st August 1953.

ROBERT F BONNER

First published 1988

© 1988 Robert F. Bonner

© Photographs: Greater Manchester Fire Service Museum; Manchester Evening News; City Engineers Dept.; Merryweather & Sons Ltd.; Central Reference Library, and others.

Published by   Archive Publications Ltd.,
Carrington Business Park,
Urmston,
Manchester M41 4DD

Production by Richardson Press.

Designed by Clive Hardy.

ACKNOWLEDGEMENTS

The author and publishers would like to thank the following institutions and individuals for their help with information and photographs for use in this book: Archives Department, Manchester Central Library; Local History Department, Manchester Central Library; City of Salford Archives Department; Chetham's School Reference Library; Committe Clerks Department, Manchester City Council; Cultural Services Department; City Engineers Department; Leyland Trucks; Manchester Evening News; Norwich Union Insurance Group; Phoenix Assurance Co. Ltd.; Sun Alliance and London Insurance Group; Guardian Royal Exchange Group; Institution of Fire Engineers; Greater Manchester Fire Service; Greater Manchester Police; the Port of Manchester Authority; Manchester Registry Office; Alice and Beatrice Craven; J. Hain; C. W. Heaps; C. C. Ashton.

CONTENTS

Foreword	5	The Blitz	76
The Insurance Brigades	6	Rebirth	92
The Fire Engine Establishment	16	The Final Years	103
Mr. Superintendent Rose	22	"Postscript" - The GMC Fire Service	119
Reorganisation	35	Major Events	125
The New Headquarters	50	Roll of Honour	126
A Police Brigade	66	Fire Stations	127

FOREWORD

A. J. Parry, MIFireE,

County Fire Officer,

Greater Manchester County Fire Service

Traditionally, the name of Manchester has always been synonymous with the highest standards of excellence in the world of firefighting, and I am therefore very pleased to be able to introduce this historical account of the Manchester Fire Brigade.

The Fire Services of Manchester have developed against a background of enormous industrial and domestic fire risk, beginning at the time of the town's awakening during the Industrial Revolution, through the Cottonopolis years, to the City's present position as a major capital. Manchester became the first Municipal Fire Service in England, the first wholly professional Brigade and a leading authority in fire prevention and firefighting technology. Its firefighters, led by a succession of dedicated and determined Chief Officers, acquired an early reputation for skill and professionalism which became renowned the world over.

In 1974, as a result of Local Government re-organisation, the City's firefighters joined with their colleagues from neighbouring towns to form a new firefighting force, known as the Greater Manchester County Fire Service, which continued the pioneering spirit of the old Brigade, and is, I am proud to say, still one of the most progressive Brigades in the country today.

The new Fire Authority is very aware of the high risk of fire in the County and ensures through the provision of personnel, stations, equipment and other resources, that the large number of emergencies that occur each year are dealt with rapidly and efficiently.

As the present Chief Officer for the Manchester conurbation, I know the strong sense of tradition and pride felt by the City's firefighters which stems directly from the Brigade's long and noble history. This book records that story in vivid detail and serves as a fine tribute to the men and women of the Manchester Fire Brigade from the earliest times to the present day.

A. J. Parry, MIFireE, County Fire Officer.

Chapter One

THE INSURANCE BRIGADES

"We have some mills in Manchester no less than nine storeys high and not one fire engine in the town that would play with effect to more than half their height."

PHOENIX FIRE OFFICE
12th December 1801

The first recorded mention of fire precautions in Manchester is to be found in the records of the Court Leet, the manorial court which functioned as a crude form of local government for nearly three hundred years. The Court, meeting on 2nd October 1566, decreed that stacks of gorse, used to fire bakehouse ovens, were to be stored at a safe distance from the premises, to prevent sparks from the oven setting them alight. The actual order reads:

"Also yt ys Ordered that all maner pson and persons kepinge eny back house within the towne of Mamchr shall not laye any Gorses or Kiddes within two bayes of the oven or Ovens."

The distance was increased in 1590 to ten yards from the nearest building, and in 1613 to one hundred yards.

Other orders forbade persons to lay "myddinges" and straw in the streets (which could be ignited by hot ashes), and banned the use of dangerous chimneys, or the lighting of fires in rooms with no chimney at all.

A more positive step, taken by the Jury in October 1615, resulted in Manchester's first fire equipment being purchased. In most of the towns and cities in Britain it has taken a serious conflagration to shock the local authorities into the provision of fire-fighting appliances; such a disaster striking at an early age meant that Manchester became equipped with fire apparatus long before many other places.

Because of this fire, described as "a great and dangerous mysfortune" that placed "the inhabitants of ye wholle towne . . . in greate danger", the Jury decreed that six ladders, twenty-four buckets, four ropes and four hooks be provided by means of a special tax. The public conduit was also ordered to be repaired at the same time.

The conduit, Manchester's only water supply, was an open pipe feeding water from the natural springs in the area now known appropriately as Spring Gardens and Fountain Street, and was established in the sixteenth century; its suitability for fire-fighting purposes is doubtful, but it is all there was.

The account books of the Constables of the Court Leet show payments for "mending the town's buckets". But in the days before fire engines were invented, to say nothing of the intricacies of modern communication systems or professional fire fighters, what was needed was a means of discovering outbreaks of fire while they were still small enough to be dealt with. Progress was made in 1636 when the Court Leet appointed two watchmen to walk the streets from 10 pm to 4 am, for the better discovery of fire and other mishaps. The watchmen were issued with hand bells in 1653 and were re-appointed every October to patrol the town during the winter months. It was apparently successful, for in 1677 the Court was able to announce that the town "hath been wonderfully preserved from fire and other acts which hath happened in several parts of this kingdom."

The public services which the Court Leet could provide were limited by the funds available and on a number of occasions help was given from the church; in 1699 Manchester's first actual fire engines were provided in this manner. The two "watar Ingans to Quench fire", purchased in London for twenty pounds plus £2.6.0 carriage, were kept at the Lodge of the Church Yard where they remained for about a hundred years.

Exactly what kind of machines these were may never be known. The fire engine was at a fairly early stage of its development and it seems certain that they were small primitive appliances, too early to be horse-drawn, and quite probably without wheels at all. Some accounts, in fact, show that Manchester's first fire engines had to be "carted" to the scene in case of fire. The pumps would be manually-operated, by means of handles, which was the only method of working until the middle of the nineteenth century.

There is evidence to suggest that the 1699 fire engines were of differing sizes. The Constables' Accounts clearly show that the first *three* engines were referred to as the "Great", "Little" and "Mean" engines;

"*5th November 1743* Joseph Wrigley for repairing the Great Engine 12s 3d"

"*2nd April 1755* Porters repairing Little Engine and for oil 1s 0d"

"*13th September 1755* Thomas Radford mending Mean Engine pipe £1 1s 0d"

Constables' Accounts from 1743 onwards show that considerable advances had been made. Certain men, described as "porters" were now receiving regular monthly payments of ten shillings for "playing at the Engines", the word 'playing' referring to the act of operating the pump, in this case for test purposes.

The Accounts show frequent disbursements for maintenance of the engines and buckets and, in 1744, for "Oyling leathern pipes", which shows that leather fire hose was being used in Manchester. Canvas hose was not to appear for about another two hundred years.

Evidence of fires having been attended is shown in the Constables' Accounts too. Ten shillings was received from the Sun Fire Office in the year 1743/44 "for use of engines". The premises on fire would have been insured with the Sun and the money paid to cover the expenses of sending engines and men.

From 1752, the "porters" are referred to as "Enginemen". It should be appreciated that at this stage there was no "fire brigade" as such in Manchester. There were merely a number of engines and other implements, belonging to the town, and certain individuals who could be called upon to operate them.

With the acquisition of a third fire appliance (the Mean engine) it seems that the Old Church Yard was now no longer large enough to house the growing fleet. Some additional accommodation was needed if the three engines were to be looked after properly and at first this took the form of rented premises.

Mention of an engine house is first made in 1744:

"*29th September* Mr. Croxton, 2 years rent for engine house to this day £4"

The engine house was, of course, kept under lock and key and on those infrequent occasions when the engines were needed for a fire would have to be opened up. With no organised fire brigade, nor any person responsible for managing the enginemen, security of the key could be a problem. An interesting entry in 1755 shows the state of affairs:

"Writing a notice upon the Engine door to find the key 2s 0d"

Before 1826 Manchester fire engines were regularly moved around the town in an endeavour to find permanent engine houses. What must have been the first purpose-built premises were constructed in 1770, when an engine house was built by Thomas Townley in the yard of the Angel public house, Market Place.

The administration meted out by the Court Leet, via the Constables and other officials, was proving to be difficult for the needs of a growing town like Manchester. It functioned in a rather medieval fashion and its legal standing was somewhat doubtful. In addition, the number of matters with which the Court Leet had to deal seemed to increase until it became difficult to cope. What was needed was a firmer basis for local government, with the backing of real legislative powers to provide the necessary public services in the town, including the fire fighting arrangements.

This materialised in 1765 with the passing of the Manchester and Salford Police Act. The Act appointed a number of named men, to be known as Commissioners, and gave them wide powers. Incorporated into it were some of the measures that had been taken by the Court Leet regarding bakehouse fuel and chimneys.

Those concerning the provision of fire engines seem quite a step forward. The Commissioners could nominate and appoint "Keepers and Managers of Fire Engines, and so many able bodied Men, not exceeding fifty, to be Firemen within the said Townships", and fix their wages. This is the first mention in Manchester of the word "firemen"; previously the term "enginemen" suggested that the men were merely hired hands to work the pumps. Provision was also made in the Act to purchase fire engines, leather buckets "and other Matters and Things relating thereto", as well as to secure a "proper and convenient Place or Places" in which to house them.

The other main feature, from a fire fighting point of view, gave powers to the Commissioners to procure water for fire fighting by breaking up any pavement or water pipe lying beneath. The only proviso was that at least one Commissioner had to be present to give the order to the firemen!

The Act also empowered the Commissioners to install "fire-plugs" in the water mains, so as to more conveniently supply the engines with water. The fixing of permanent plugs - holes in the pipes for access into which a wooden plug was hammered - would avoid having to break open pavements and mains indiscriminately.

All this promised an era of efficiency and improved status; unfortunately little seems to have been actually done. The fire engines and enginemen remained under the control of the Court Leet, the Constables continuing to pay their wages, and the water supply still remained rather primitive.

However some action was taken with regard to purchasing new appliances and providing engine houses for them. Within five years the Constables were able to publish the following notice in the local press:

"*Manchester, October 9th 1770*
The inhabitants of this Town, are desired to take notice, that the old Engines for extinguishing Fire, are at the Lodge in the *Old Church Yard* and in the Engine House, *Tib Lane,* as heretofore; that one new smaller Engine is at *St. John's* Church, a second at *St. Mary's,* a third in the *Angel Yard, Market Place,* a fourth at *Mr.Josiah Birch's, High Street,* and a fifth at *Deputy*

Kay's, Milngate where they are kept in constant readiness and the Constables beg this opportunity of requesting all Manner of Persons to be most careful in preventing the Necessity of using them."

Although the Enginemen remained under the control of the Constables, there is a subtle change in the Account books after 1765 which suggests that another aspect of the Police Act had materialised. From this time, regular payments of enginemen's "wages" are described, incidentally never much higher than one guinea per month between them. Side by side with wage bills are payments for ale, a frequent reward for pumping assistants at the time, and other sundries which show that they were still treated as somewhat casual employees:

"*21st January 1772*   Enginemen for extraordinary trouble 2s 6d"

"*4th July 1773*   To Drink for the engine men as encouragement 1s 6d"

The Manchester Directory for 1781 uses the term "firemen" in a description of fire protection arrangements, and actually names them as Thomas Bewley (Clerk to the Insurance Office), James Batty (Dep. Constable), Jonathan Brown, John Falkner, John Heathcote, Isaac Hewit, George Salt, Henry Smith and James Thompson. This is the earliest record of named firemen in Manchester. The same directory gives a list of eight engines, which matches that given in the 1770 Constables' notice. This amounts to less than two men per engine and sufficient hands to operate the pumps would be obtained from the crowd, no doubt on the promise of liquid refreshment.

The reference to Mr. Bewley as being "Clerk to the Insurance Office" is noteworthy, as the first intimations of active fire insurance operations in Manchester appear at this time. Fire insurance in Britain began soon after the Great Fire of London in 1666, and by the end of the seventeenth century, the Hand-in-Hand Office became the first to operate a fire engine and corps of men to protect its interests.

Some years later, in 1771, a local company, the Manchester Fire Office, was formed. A surviving policy of the Manchester Fire Office bears an illustration depicting a small manual fire engine and two uniformed figures with firefighting implements. This would appear to suggest the existence of a company fire brigade, possibly the earliest in Manchester. The policy is signed by the Clerk, Thomas Bewley, who was a Manchester fireman, and so adds to the circumstantial evidence of insurance fire brigade operation in the town at this time. The Manchester was acquired in 1788 by the Phoenix Assurance Company, a younger company established only in 1782. By 1785 they had a full-time representative in Manchester, Mr. William Tate Junior, with an office at Star Yard, Deansgate. The Phoenix does not appear to have had its own fire brigade in Manchester, choosing instead to make donations to improve fire precautions.

In February 1788 a fire engine and twenty-four buckets were presented to the Town. The following year the same company contributed £25 towards the installation of fire plugs. These would have been supplied from the waterworks system of Sir Oswald Mosley, taking water from the River Medlock. By 1794 eleven such plugs had been installed, situated in Market Cross, Hyde's Cross, Dangerous Corner, Apple Market, Hanging Ditch, Cannon Street, three on Deansgate, St. Ann's Square and Market Street Lane.

In 1794 there were, apart from the Phoenix, three other company agents in the town. These were the Liverpool in Back King Street, the Royal Exchange in Exchange Street, and the Sun, which, in addition to having its agency office at King Street, also had a fire engine. The engine, referred to as No. 11 in a list of eleven Manchester fire engines published in the 1794 Directory, was kept at Hatters Lane, and its "Conductor" is named as a Miss Plant. Elizabeth Plant had taken over the agency following the death of her father, and she held office for four years until being succeeded by Robert Duck in September 1796. Unfortunately there is no evidence of her having attended any fires during that period and the image conjured up of a bold young lady, resplendent in the blue tunic and white breeches of the Sun Office fire brigade, and "conducting" operations at a Manchester fire, though tempting, is unlikely. Company agents would be chosen for their administrative ability rather than for any smoke eating qualities and the bestowing of the title "Conductor" on Miss Plant was probably more of an honorary measure. Robert Duck, who is known to have attended some fires, apparently also held the post of Scavenger for the Market Street area. As well as actually operating a fire brigade, the Sun made financial gifts to the town in the same way as the other companies, assisting with the provision of better fire plugs, for instance, which would benefit their own operations as well.

Two more company brigades are known to have operated in Manchester, though a little later than this; these being the Norwich Union and the Royal Exchange. Meanwhile the authority's own firefighting arrangements showed further progress. By 1794 there were ten engines, a Conductor in charge of each, plus a number of firemen allocated to him, varying from one to three. There was also an "Inspector of the Fire Engines", Francis Taylor, whose job was to take care of the equipment.

A new Manchester and Salford Police Act of 1792 replaced the earlier legislation. An important addition decreed that all new buildings were to have fourteen inch party walls between occupancies, extending from the foundations, through all storeys, to twelve inches above the roof, to limit the spread of fire. In practice, several buildings were erected without the necessary separation, despite the provisions of the Police Act.

The word "Police" in this context does not mean what it does today. It was more of a general term referring to the various public services of watching, lighting, firefighting and so on which were under the control of the "Police Commissioners". In later years the word "watch" - and nowadays the phrase "public protection" - had similar connotations.

Seven years after the passing of the new Act, sweeping changes were made in the town's firefighting arrangements. On 27th December 1799 the Commissioners, meeting at the Police Office, ordered that twenty-two firemen be appointed "for the ensuing year", to include the Beadles and the Turncock, a Mr. Isaac Perrins. Just what qualifications the Beadles, or indeed any of the others, had for the job is doubtful. Perrins, who was to be the "Inspector of Engines and Conductor of Firemen", and thus in charge of the fire brigade, did have some of the qualities of leadership. A man of many parts, his chief claim to fame was as a prize-fighter, having been one of the leading bare-knuckle exponents of the day.

Described as "a man who to a lionlike strength of body united the disposition of a lamb", the 6'2", seventeen-stone Perrins was no doubt the sort of man suited to being a fire chief in 1799, if not today!

Lock-ups at the Police Office were converted into an engine house, and a Conductor was appointed for each of the ten engines, under Perrins' overall control. Interestingly, these Conductors included the Agents of the Sun and Royal Exchange offices, suggesting a measure of public control over the Insurance engines.

Uniform, consisting of coats and japanned caps, was provided and the engines brought up to a state of good repair. A board was installed over each fireman's house to show watchmen and others where the firemen lived, and it was also ordered that the fire plugs be taken up and frames installed, to avoid digging up the pavement. The twenty-two firemen received wages of three guineas per year, while

Perrins was awarded an annual salary of £20; unfortunately he did not live long enough to draw more than one year's payment. On the evening of Wednesday 10th December 1800, there broke out in the centre of Manchester the worst fire that anybody could remember. It started in a warehouse building in Hodson's Square, which was destroyed in less than an hour, together with the whole of Kinder's Court. That buildings in Market Street Lane, Cannon Street and the Market Place were not also consumed was probably due more to a change of wind direction during the night than to the skill of the firefighters. The small manual engines were useless in dealing with blazing warehouses stocked with cotton, and efforts were directed to preserving the adjacent property. Soldiers of the 4th Dragoons and the Manchester Volunteers were called in to assist but the exertions of firefighting were too much for the fifty-year-old Perrins. He caught a serious illness as a result of the fire and died on 6th January. At least three other persons suffered the same fate, and the press aptly referred to it all as "the fire fever".

After the incident, the firemen came in for a lot of criticism from a stunned public, though perhaps unfairly so. The Boroughreeve and Constables felt obliged to issue a public notice, repudiating claims that the engines had been in disrepair at the time of the fire.

The loss caused by this fire was estimated at over £50,000, a considerable sum in those days, and not including the looting which went on afterwards.

Before a successor to Isaac Perrins could be found, an even more horrific fire struck, on 27th January, which carried the highest-ever death toll in any Manchester building fire to date. It occurred at Kirby and Littlewood's linen yarn factory, beside the River Medlock near to Oxford Road, and a staggering 23 lives were lost. Most of the victims were boys and girls, little more than children, who had been sent out to work by poor parents. The majority of children were trapped on the topmost floor, access to which was via a ladder and trap door. Three or

Manchester Fire Insurance Company firemark.

four girls jumped to their deaths, and one young boy was seen hanging by his hands from a beam until he fell into the heart of the fire.

"A more heart-rending sight was never witnessed", said the Gazette, "several of the unfortunate children were seen running through the flames in a state of distraction, without the most distant possibility of escaping". The firemen were powerless to save either the occupants or the building. Clearly a fire brigade without a chief was in no shape to deal with such serious fires.

The Commissioners appointed a successor to the unfortunate Perrins in March 1801. The man chosen was Thomas Knight, with the same salary of £20 per year. At the same time the number of firemen was increased to twenty-five.

For some reason the chief qualification for Conductor of the Fire Engines in Manchester at the beginning of the nineteenth century seemed to be an ability to repair the engines. Perrins had been an engineer and sent several repair bills for work done on the fire engines. This policy was to prove itself to the Commissioners as a mistake, but not before a string of dubious characters had passed through the job. Thomas Knight was an engineer and blacksmith, and was also involved with repairs to the Police engines.

Fire brigade operations in Thomas Knight's day were usually hampered by two main problems. Firstly the lack of full-time firemen, or a satisfactory means of turning them out, meant that a building was usually well alight when they arrived; secondly the water supplies were inadequate to say the least.

Feeling was mounting though towards alleviating at least one of these problems. The Police Commissioners, who already had control of the sewers, were particularly anxious to obtain the waterworks from the Lord of the Manor. In the end a private Act of Parliament was secured by a new firm, known as the Manchester and Salford Waterworks Company. The Company set out to replace the old system and lay a network of stone pipes, though nobody could have envisaged the fraudulent way in which this would be carried out.

It transpired that the Waterworks Company was formed by a number of directors of another firm, the Stone Pipe Company, with whom they contracted for the supply of pipes; in other words, they were selling pipes to themselves. The pipes were of soft, porous sandstone, totally useless for the job for which they were intended, and yet the Company was apparently well aware of this. Work started in 1810 and the mains were laid in such a manner, in different parts of the town, that discovery of their uselessness could not be made until the scheme was almost completed.

The first test was made in July 1812 when the Sub Engineer turned water into an 18 inch section of main: it fractured immediately; subsequent tests resulted in further bursts.

A recommendation that stone pipes be used only in the high parts of Manchester where the pressure would not exceed thirty to forty feet, was apparently ignored.

The Company felt able to announce in 1813 that they could supply water in certain streets. However sufficient quantities for firefighting could not be guaranteed. In 1814 the Commissioners appointed a special committee which decided that new fire wells should be sunk in various streets. By 1817 there were twelve such wells. At the same time new fire plugs were fixed into the stone water mains. Unfortunately it was to be several more years before a *constant* supply of water could be guaranteed. As it was the mains were dry for much of the time, and in the event of fire the turncock would have to divert the water to wherever it was required. An entry in the Manchester Directories of the period reads:

"*TURNCOCK*: Alexander Duthie, 16 Tib Street, to whom application may be made in case of fire".

It was hardly surprising that fires often burned themselves out while waiting for water.

A new Act of 1816 required the Waterworks

Section of stone water pipe excavated in Sackville Street, 1972.

Company to fix fire plugs in all new mains and to deliver keys for them to each engine house, or any insurance office which requested them.

Meanwhile the old Waterworks Company had gone into liquidation and an 1823 Act prohibited any director to be concerned in contracts for the supply of articles for the waterworks, or to make any profit from such a contract. After the disappearance of the old Company, Manchester was eventually supplied with water via iron pipes from the Gorton reservoirs.

By this time Thomas Knight was long gone. He was dismissed in March 1812 "in consequence of his conduct on the occasion of the recent fire". This incident was probably the Sunday afternoon blaze at Haigh, Marshall and Tideswell's warehouse in High Street on 9th February which caused £100,000 worth of damage. Unfortunately the nature of Knight's crime is not recorded. In his place, the Commissioners appointed William Vickers, a coppersmith and brassfounder, who had done repair work on the engines and so was no doubt considered to be adequately qualified for the post. Instructions were given to the Constables to "take the care of the fire engines belonging to the town", and also

> "that the oldest fire Engine be repaired thoroughly and placed upon wheels similar to those belonging to the fire engine Marked No. 1".

During the eight years in which William Vickers was Conductor certain limited progress was made.

In December 1819 the Commissioners accepted the offer of the re-formed Waterworks Company to supply water for firefighting, and ordered connection to be made with the fire wells. Another development came in January when the Commissioners authorised their Fire Engine Committee to "appoint an efficient body of Firemen to each Engine with distinguishing badges". They also empowered the Committee to appoint and dismiss firemen, and to draw up rules and regulations for their conduct. The last item did not in fact materialise until 1822 when a set of rules was finalised.

William Vickers left in disgrace in 1820, following an investigation by the Commissioners into irregularities in the accounts.

In accordance with normal practice, the Commissioners decided to cure their problems by increasing the number of firemen - this time to 35 - and replacing the Conductor with another suitably-qualified tradesman. The new man was Phineas Sykes, a cooper from Deansgate, who had been repairing fire engine buckets for many years, though he was not, of course, a fireman. It was also ordered at this time that such Beadles as were employed as firemen be discharged and that no more Beadles be appointed as such in future.

The report concerning William Vickers revealed the lack of confidence which at least one insurance office had in the Department. In glowing terms, the Fire Engine Committee stated the willingness of the Royal Exchange Insurance Company to take back the fire engine which it had previously presented to the town, maintain the appliance and provide the men to operate it. The Committee even went on to say that this would be an advantage to Manchester and implored the Commissioners to not only accede, but to recommend to the other 5 offices, which had donated engines, that they do the same. The Committee must have had little faith in their own brigade and its Conductors if they were so willing to hand over to private enterprise. In the event only the Royal Exchange engine was given back and the Department remained as it was, plodding on towards reorganisation in 1826.

The Royal kept its brigade for several more years. In 1825 the firm advertised for a new engine house and the brigade continued in operation until 1831 when financial reasons forced its closure. By then there would be adequate alternatives in Manchester.

The other company brigade which was very active at this time, and earning regular accolades was the Norwich Union, believed to have been formed around 1814 by the Company's agents Messrs. Higson and Hughes of King Street. The Conductor of the Norwich Brigade was Peter Taylor, who held the post for over twenty years until the brigade was disbanded. Following this he became a messenger with the company. On the occasion of his funeral, on Christmas Day 1840, the full complement of the Manchester (Police) Fire Establishment, together with a fire engine, took part in the procession through the town to St. George's Church, Hulme, a fitting gesture to a man who, after all, had been in his own right Chief Officer of one of Manchester's most efficient fire brigades.

Opinion of the Norwich brigade seems to have been higher than that of the Police Commissioners' firemen. When a fire destroyed the warehouse of Messrs. Clay and Cullingworth in Marsden Square, Wheeler's Manchester Chronicle reported that "the various engines soon arrived, the admirable one of the Norwich Union Office being, as usual, the first at the post of danger".

A fire in Portland Street in 1821 also saw the Brigade arriving first, "with its characteristic alacrity". The owner of the cotton factory adjoining the building on fire was full of praise for the "judicious and very effective manner in which their engine was conducted", resulting in his own premises escaping completely unscathed.

A comprehensive set of rules was framed by the Norwich for its firemen, which showed that their staff were well-disciplined. Fines were imposed for drunkenness, fighting and misuse of uniform, and the men were arrayed in green and red, with low crowned hats, jackboots and silver arm-badges. A red jacket, worn by a postilion in the Norwich's Manchester Brigade, is displayed in the firm's museum. The Company's engine house was at St. Peter's Fields, where the men had to parade monthly for inspection; horses were hired from Shaw's livery stables in Mosley Street.

In many respects the private fire brigade of the Norwich Union was much more advanced than anything the Police Commissioners could provide. This was in no small way due to the comparatively better financial position of a firm such as the Norwich. As things turned out, it was to be the insurance companies - or rather their money - which provided the key to the formulation of a bold new scheme which gave Manchester a first-class municipal fire service at little or no extra expense.

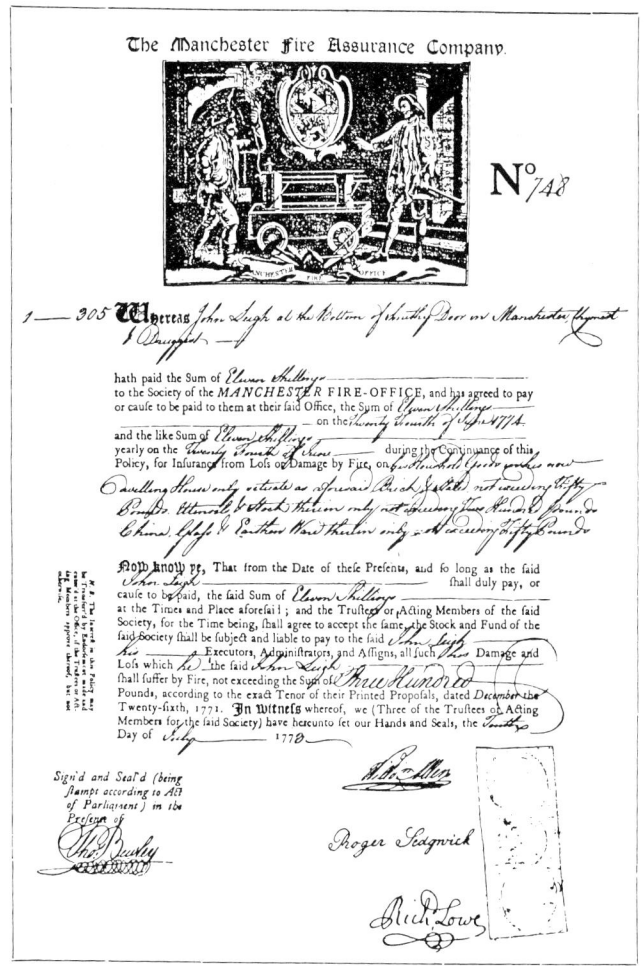

MINIATURE OF POLICY ISSUED IN 1773

Manchester Fire Assurance Co. policy, 1773. The Clerk, Thomas Bewley (lower left signature) was also a Manchester fireman.

15

Chapter Two

THE FIRE ENGINE ESTABLISHMENT

"... the adoption of regularity, instead of the old mode of acting without any".

MANCHESTER MERCURY

22nd November 1825

Phineas Sykes lasted for nearly two years as Conductor of the Fire Engine Department before being discharged for an unrecorded reason. His successor was Richard Downing, who was soon repairing engines and supplying equipment like his predecessors, despite a new ruling to the contrary.

On Downing's appointment in 1822 the Department had thirty-five firemen, all part-time, and 14 engines, located at the Police Yard, Water Street; Collier's Yard, Duke Street; Simpson's Factory, Miller Street and the Infirmary.

The engine houses were not lavish structures by any means. The premises in Mr. Collier's yard had been built in 1820 for £14-10-0 with an annual rent of one guinea being payable "with liberty to take away the building materials if it should become necessary by a notice to quit the premises".

Under Downing's management, the Department moved a little nearer to a state of efficiency, and certain advancements were made. The engines were kept in good repair, and new clothing purchased for the men. Land was acquired at Clarence Street in 1822 for the erection of a new Police Yard and central engine house, which became occupied about 1825.

In November 1822, the Fire Engine Committee presented a set of rules for the Conductor and firemen, the first such ever drawn up in Manchester, and the Police Commissioners adopted the code without alteration. It read:

"RULES FOR THE CONDUCT OF THE SUPERINTENDENT OR CONDUCTOR OF THE FIRE ENGINE DEPARTMENT OF THE MANCHESTER POLICE.

1st He must take charge of the engine, pipes, carts, draught, plugs and all other apparatus connected with them, and see that the engines are properly equipped and always in perfect working order.

2nd He must see that the Sub-Conductors of engines and the firemen do their duty at *all* times and take especial care that the engines and pipes are well oiled and attended in all respects as early as possible after a fire has taken place, and make his report of the same, and of all necessary repairs which may be wanted; and also report as to the conduct of the Sub-Conductors and Firemen and submit the same to the Committee, at their monthly meeting together with any other matter or thing which may be deemed requisite.

RULES AND REGULATIONS TO BE OBSERVED BY THE FIREMEN BELONGING TO THE MANCHESTER POLICE

1st That every fireman shall appear in full uniform and clean on every day appointed for the purpose of inspecting the engines, pipes, etc. and on any particular occasion when directed to attend. Any one absent when the roll is called over, or not in uniform and clean shall be fined for each offence one shilling.

2nd That any fireman absenting himself from any fire shall be fined five shillings, unless he can produce satisfactory reasons for such absence.

3rd That any fireman attending any fire or any other duty in a state of intoxication shall be fined two shillings and sixpence.

4th That the Conductor of each engine shall keep the same clean and in good order as well as the pipes and all other matters belonging thereunto, any neglect of this duty shall subject him to a fine of two shillings and sixpence.

5th That any fireman neglecting to attend to assist the Conductor in cleaning the engines, pipes, &c, when called upon shall be fined two shillings and sixpence.

6th That any fireman wearing any part of his uniform, except on duty, shall be fined one shilling.

7th That any fireman going to any insurance or other office or to any person whatever to ask or demand money or payment for attendance at any fire shall be fined five shillings.

MEMORANDUM The above fines to be under the direction of the Committee who shall have a discretionary power as to encreasing or alleviating the fines as they may think right on view of the case."

The most significant development, however, was to take place in the next three to four years, and began in March 1824 when a group of people meeting in King Street resolved unanimously to form a new fire and life company; one month later the Manchester Fire and Life Assurance Company (which had no connections with the old Manchester Fire Assurance Company) was launched.

By 1825 the Company had a fire brigade in Liverpool which had an excellent reputation. The *Manchester Courier* for October carried a story of a Mr. Hewitt, trunk maker of Lord Street, Liverpool, whose shop was under a warehouse. Smelling smoke one day, he called in the Manchester Assurance Brigade who sent a fireman to investigate. The fireman found nothing amiss but advised Mr. Hewitt to insure his shop with the Manchester. Without further ado, the shopkeeper repaired to the agency to insure his premises for £100. The agent persuaded him to make it £200 which was agreed to, and before the proverbial ink was dry, the building burnt down! The office paid in full.

That year the Company appointed a Committee to consider the advantages of forming their own fire brigade in Manchester. From discussions with the Deputy Constable and the Controller at the Police Office, the Committee found there was already dissatisfaction in the town with the existing arrangements. There were too many engines, not enough firemen, and the wages paid were inadequate. The Commissioners were apparently unwilling to provide any more public money for fire protection and the best way forward seemed to be for the Company to "induce" the Commissioners to provide an improved system financed by contributions from the Insurance companies; alternatively, the Manchester office would have to set up its own fire brigade. A number of Directors of the Company were also Police Commissioners, and these were urged to attend the June meeting to promote the proposal. If adopted, it would result in an improved Fire Engine Department with no increase in public expenditure. At the same time the Company's clients would enjoy the benefits of an efficient fire brigade without the initial expense of the firm forming their own establishment.

The idea was so simple and workable that it is surprising nobody had thought of it before. All that apparently remained was to persuade fellow Offices to contribute and proceed with the reorganisation. The proposal came not before time at a meeting of the Commissioners on July 13th. It was said that at almost every fire, the utmost disorder and confusion prevailed, due entirely to the want of a person of sufficient authority to control the firemen.

"Disorder and confusion" was by no means an overstatement. At a recent incident involving Mr. Drew's grocery shop, Smithy Door, the building was well alight on arrival. A full forty-five minutes elapsed before water could be obtained from the street mains and by this time, the shop, together with the adjacent one, had been destroyed. A third shop and a public house were also involved to a lesser degree. Several hours later, during damping down operations, the firemen turned their jets onto the crowd, who were trying to get into the ruins to look for money. The response was predictable. In the ensuing affray, a brick was thrown which hit Thomas Booth, Collector of the Waterworks rate, knocking him unconscious. Whether this was intended for the firemen in return for drenching the onlookers or for Mr. Booth, whose Company was in no small way responsible for the delay in fire-fighting operations, is a matter on which local newspapers differ, but does not really matter. The attacker was arrested by a police watchman and later £85 was found in the ruins.

When fire broke out in the yard of Sharp, Hill & Co's power-loom factory in Falkner Street one Sunday afternoon in July, the *Manchester Guardian* commented that

> "whatever difference of opinion may exist as to the origin of the fire, we believe there is none as to the utter inefficiency of the means employed to extinguish it. Complaints of the misconduct of the firemen, and of their utter want of a system in the management of the engines, are in the mouths of everyone who witnessed their proceedings; and we trust no time will now be lost in removing the imputation which has lain upon Manchester for many years, of having the worst regulated and most inefficient fire police of any town in the United Kingdom."

At almost every fire it seemed that the engines either arrived too late, or else were unable to obtain water. Even when these problems did not arise, then the firemen worked haphazardly and apparently without supervision. When the engines of more than one Office were in attendance at the same fire, there was no co-operation.

At a fire in a multi-occupancy building in Bridgewater Street on 11th October 1825, the *Manchester Mercury* observed:-

> "One of the Police Engines arrived at the spot very soon after the fire was discovered, but for want of hands it could not be made available. Another Engine, belonging to one of the Fire Offices arrived about half an hour afterwards, and great complaints are made of the conduct of the firemen who accompanied it".

The paper went on to say that:-

> "This case affords another instance of having *all* the engines under the direction of one or two cool and intelligent persons under whose orders it should be imperative on the firemen to act. If such a system had been in existence now, and the engines rendered available immediately on their arrival, there is little doubt that much of the loss in the present instance might have been prevented".

Whether or not the Mercury knew it, just such a system was being planned. On 2nd November, a "Plan for the better regulating and conducting of the Fire Engine Department of the Police of the Town", was laid before the General Meeting of Commissioners.

The recommendations of the Committee included the appointment of a "clever, intelligent and active man, conversant with the general principles of engineering", as Superintendent, who would take full charge of all men and equipment for £100 per annum plus a rent-free house adjacent to the Police Yard.

The firemen would receive four guineas a year and at least six were also to reside close to the yard, ready for immediate turnout. It was also proposed that, as the Superintendent would not be fully occupied in his fire brigade duties, his "leisure time" should be employed in some other task "where his services may be useful".

In case of fire, the Superintendent and men would be "entitled" to claim from the insurance offices, or uninsured property owners, allowances of between 6d and 4/- per hour. Other recommendations provided for the erection of fire stations, bells and signs to indicate the fire plugs.

The plan was agreed to unanimously, and the Committee empowered to take steps for carrying it into effect, including advertising for a Superintendent following the resignation of Downing.

The next General Meeting of Commissioners was on Wednesday 16th November and got off to a sombre start. Boroughreeve, William Lomas, in the chair, announced that the police funds were overdrawn to the tune of £17,000, and that the bank had refused further payments unless steps were taken to reduce this overdraft. A worse moment to launch a new fire service could not have been envisaged. Nevertheless, after considerable discussion the Commissioners passed the following resolutions:-

"That the Fire Engine Establishment of the Police is at present ill calculated to afford adequate protection to the property of the inhabitants and it is highly expedient that some measure should be adopted for putting it on a more efficient footing.

That an amended system be carried into effect, provided the Committee may be able by means of arrangements to be made with the different Fire Insurance Offices having establishments in this town or by any other means to confine the whole of the expence of the Fire Engine establishment chargeable on the Police Funds,- within its existing amount; a limitation which the present state of those funds renders imperiously necessary".

In addition, the Committee was empowered to appoint a Superintendent, and thirty-six firemen at the recommended salaries, eight of the firemen to be designated Captains, for an extra guinea per year. It was to be a condition that the Superintendent should "devote to the Fire Engine Establishment the whole or such portion of his time as the Committee may require, and shall perform such duties as they may prescribe for him". A further resolution required the Committee to frame a code of regulations for the Superintendent and firemen, "for procuring order whenever fires may occur", and the Committee was also empowered to purchase any necessary equipment, except new engines.

The Fire Engine Committee met again on December 14th 1825, to study the testimonials of the candidates for the position of Superintendent, and unanimously chose Monmouthshire-born Captain Charles Anthony RN. His service record was admirable. Joining the Navy in 1792, in his sixteenth year, he served on the "Russell", and took part in the defeat of the French at Ushant. After being involved in many successful naval battles he later served in Canada where he was present at the taking of Niagara and planned the construction of the one-hundred gun "Ontario". In 1813 he was promoted Commander for his part in the capture of Oswego and returned to England two years later.

Captain Anthony's appointment was subject to satisfactory funds being promised from the insurance offices, and the subsequent approval of the General Meeting of Commissioners.

The response from the companies varied. The Atlas agreed on December 20th via their Manchester agent Mr. James Hervey, to contribute £10 per annum "if necessary" towards a "General Engine Establishment for the Town of Manchester". The Phoenix Assurance was prepared to make an initial contribution, but did not wish to be involved in annual subscriptions. The Sun Office resolved on 9th March 1826 to subscribe £20 per annum towards the Establishment "provided that sum be understood to cover all Expences attending the extinguishing of fires". Two months later, on 11th May, the Office agreed to increase the subscription to £25 per annum, on the same condition.

Unfortunately the Sun does not appear to have actually made any contribution, despite these favourable resolutions. The Royal Exchange also agreed, on 3rd April 1826, to a £25 contribution. However, on receipt of a letter in the following October, from the Manchester Boroughreeve who found the £25 insufficient, the Fire Committee of the Company decided to withdraw its contribution and continue its own fire engine establishment.

The apparent low opinion which the Royal Exchange had of the new Engine Establishment was unfortunate. By the time this Resolution was passed, the Establishment had really been accomplished, even though it was in its infancy.

The largest contribution to the Establishment came from the firm which initiated the whole idea. On April 13th 1826, the Board of Directors of the Manchester Assurance Company considered the proposed improvement in the Fire Engine Establishment and agreed:-

"That this Company will subscribe One Hundred Pounds per annum for the above purpose on condition that the Commissioners of Police continue to contribute the Sum which appears to have been the cost of the Fire Engine Establishment on the average of the last three years, and that the new Establishment be conducted in a liberal and efficient manner".

The gratitude felt towards the Manchester Assurance Company for its part in putting the Manchester Fire Brigade on its feet was not exactly modest. An account in the *Manchester Guardian* of the fire engine procession on 1st May 1833, an annual event in the thirties, states:-

"The procession returned down Mosley Street, York Street, King Street and on coming opposite to the Manchester Assurance Company's offices, the men cheered heartily".

With further contributions promised from the London Guardian and the Beacon Offices, the Fire Engine Committee felt that there would be sufficient funds to adopt the new scheme, and to recommend Captain Anthony's appointment to the General Meeting of Commissioners. Their report was presented on May 3rd 1826 and it was explained how the "great liberality of two of the principal companies had furnished the Committee with means sufficient to enable them to commence the improved system".

The Meeting ordered that the appointment of Captain Anthony be confirmed, and thus gave birth to the new Fire Establishment.

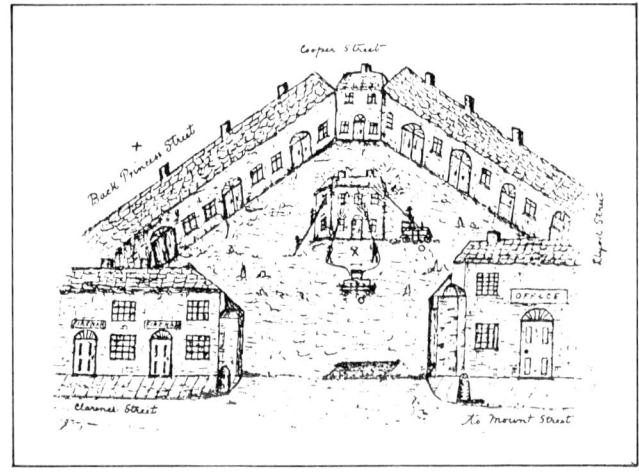

Sketch showing layout of the Town's Yard, Clarence Street, first permanent Headquarters of the Manchester Fire Brigade, and site of the present Town Hall.

Wheeled escape ladder, Town's Yard, Manchester.

Chapter Three

MR SUPERINTENDENT ROSE

"This establishment is perhaps the most effective in the Kingdom."

MANCHESTER AS IT IS

Published 1839

The existence of a municipal fire service is marked, generally, by the appointment of a paid full-time Superintendent, the ceasing of Company brigade operations, or the acceptance of financial responsibilities by the local authority. In this respect, Manchester can truly claim to have had, in 1826, the first such service in England, even though two Company brigades, the Royal Exchange and Norwich Union, continued for a few years.

In June 1826, the Fire Engine Committee reported on their suggestions for reducing the appliances. The proposals involved retaining six large horse-drawn engines and two small hand-propelled ones, and dispensing with the other seven. The reason for keeping so many was to ensure satisfactory fire cover for the whole town by having engines stationed around the area.

Following the rationalisation of the engines, little change occurred in the next two years, apart from the introduction in December 1826 of a ten shilling per mile per engine charge for over-the-border calls, plus a ten shilling per engine turnout fee.

Captain Anthony resigned on the 15th October 1827 to take up a new appointment and the Fire Engine Committee were in no doubt about the services he had rendered to the Department:-

"Before his appointment, the Establishment was notoriously inefficient, the Engines were almost unserviceable and the firemen were in a state of complete insubordination. From this state he has during the short time he held the situation brought the whole establishment into such order as renders it a credit to the town to which it belongs; whilst he himself by his uniform good conduct and gentlemanly deportment secured the esteem and respect of those who knew him."

A fine testimonial indeed to a man who had only served for eighteen months. It must be remembered though that fire brigades were still at the stage when it was more important for a chief officer to exhibit qualities of discipline and management than to have any technical knowledge of firefighting.

The resignation of Anthony left the Brigade without a leader at a time when the new system was just beginning to prove satisfactory. This could have been a disaster, but the Committee "had the good fortune" to meet a man named Thomas Gallimore, who was able to take temporary command immediately. Like Captain Anthony, Gallimore was from a service background, having been an officer in the Field Train Department of the Royal Artillery from 1806 to 1815, and had seen action at Waterloo and other battles. In the six months during which he acted as Superintendent, Mr. Gallimore appears to have given a good account of himself, and the Fire Engine Committee considered it a foregone conclusion that he would take up the post permanently. However, this was not to be and the Commissioners appointed Mr. William Rose, a horse-dealer from Salford.

Gallimore did not go quietly. In the autumn he actually applied again for the post of Superintendent, and in December he still had in his possession fire brigade books and papers including a list of all the fire plugs in the town, the absence of which caused great inconvenience to Superintendent Rose. In the end, the Commissioners paid Gallimore a quarter of a year's salary (£37-10-0) for the period in between Rose's appointment (April) and the time he was actually able to commence duties.

The exploits and innovations of William Rose and his son, Thomas, during their respective periods as Superintendent first made MFB a name synonymous with efficiency, a tradition which remained with the Brigade until the end, over a century later.

An Act of Parliament within William Rose's first years of office legalised practices which had taken place for years, such as the payment of injury awards to firemen, and the employment of assistants at fires, which thus strengthened the brigades position. In addition, the Commissioners were empowered to make charges on owners or occupiers, not exceeding £15.

Civilian pumping assistants, to operate the handles of the manual fire engines, were a normal part of firefighting until improved water supplies and steam fire engines made them obsolete. There were always difficulties in managing the labourers; a large fire in Manchester, would usually attract a number of undesirables, who frequently came on the scene looking for easy money and who often obstructed the firemen; pickpocketing was also rife. An incident in Shudehill during May of 1828 was a typical case, as the *Guardian* reported:-

"It is usual for the offices where buildings which happen to take fire are insured to pay for the assistance of men who work the engines in a day or two after the fire. And the difficulty on the present occasion to procure the necessary assistance arose from a number of men who are in the practice of attending fires to procure jobs in this way, refusing to assist on the ground that they had not been paid for their labour on the occasion of the late fire at Messrs. Peel and Company."

The problem was eased somewhat in 1830 when arm badges were purchased to be issued to assistants at fires. Any reward would then only be paid on production of the badge.

It was over the question of casual assistance at fires that the MFB had its first of several disputes with the insurance offices. The trouble arose after a fire at Windsor Bridge, Salford, in August 1829. Rose and his men attended, after which an account was sent to the Phoenix office, who refused to pay for the expenses of the assistants. The matter was taken up by the Lamps etc. Committee with the Phoenix head office, who argued that the casual assistants only contributed towards the saving of the occupier's uninsured interest, and not of the insured portion, for the loss of which they had already paid out. The Company added that the difference should be paid by the occupier. An agreement was eventually reached to prepare a scale of charges for firemen and assistants and this was confirmed by the Lamps etc. Committee on October 5th as follows:

"*FIREMEN*:-

For a turnout in the event of a fire when the engines are not used	1/- each
For the first hour working the engines	1/- each
Any succeeding half hour ditto	6d each

ASSISTANTS:-
For working the engines per hour   6d each."

No sooner had this problem been settled than a second one arose a month later, following a serious fire at a warehouse in Dale Street. The owners, the Rochdale Canal Co., refused to pay the charge as no portion of their building was saved, and insisted that the two tenants of the warehouse, Messrs. Barnby, Faulkner and Co., and the Halifax Merchants Co., should be asked to pay. The fact that the fire also destroyed all the tenants property seems to have been considered unimportant. The dispute was solved by dividing the account three ways, but such opposition remained a regular occurrence as long as the Brigade had charging powers.

The Dale Street fire caused a great destruction of property, and the death of a firefighter. It broke out around 5 am on the morning of October 12th 1829, starting in the boat loading bay underneath Messrs. Barnby's building, which straddled a canal arm, and soon took hold of the adjacent Halifax Merchants Company warehouse. £12,000 worth of cotton was consumed, though the Brigade successfully saved a nearby grain warehouse. At about 10.30 am, two Royal Exchange firemen were standing in a doorway when the building began to shake. Without really thinking, one man ran inside the building and survived as the wall collapsed, but his comrade, Thomas Taylor, was hit by falling debris as he ran out, and died from his injuries two days later.

The efforts of Manchester's firemen at such large fires were not helped by the antiquated machinery they had to use. At a blaze at Fairbairn & Lillie's, Canal Street, Ancoats, one engine leaked so badly it had to be wrapped in yarn taken from the burning building, and when a water tub was filled from a fire plug, it leaked through the staves and had to be replaced by a cask from a nearby public house. In February 1830, William Rose submitted a report, which included his recommendations to replace five old engines with one new one.

Estimates were invited from Richard Downing and he quoted £145 for an engine with 9" pumps on his "improved principle". His offer was accepted and the new engine was delivered in 1831. It was so

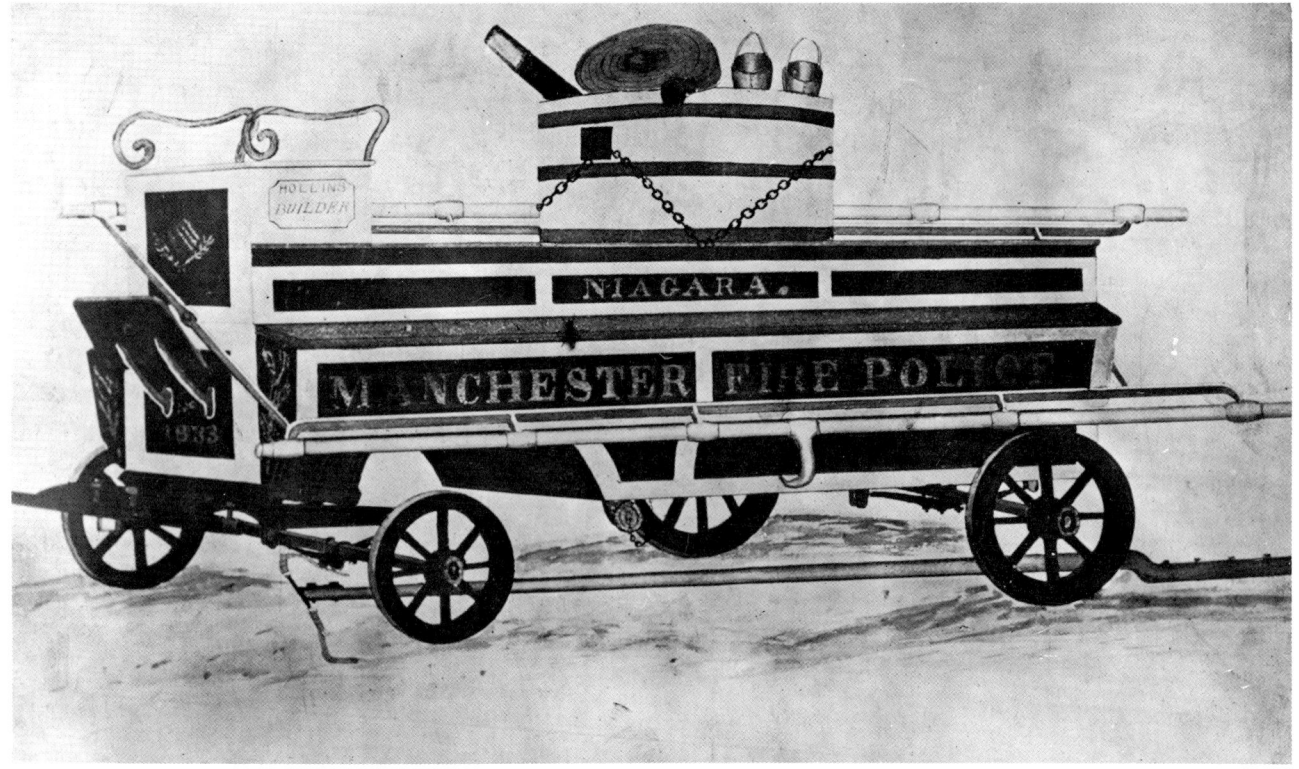

Niagara engine, 1833. One of the five locally-built Hollins manual pumps supplied in the 1830's.

successful that by 1835 four more had been commissioned. On tests, the 24-man-operated engines, weighing nearly two tons, threw water a hundred feet high.

The engines were made in Lower Mosley Street and fitted with water tubs, which meant that they could take their own water supplies to an incident, a capability taken for granted today, but virtually unheard of at the time. Appropriately, these new additions to the fleet were given splendid names such as *Water Witch* and *Niagara*.

One problem, besides the equipment, was that there was no rank structure. Reporting in July 1830, Rose suggested having a Sergeant and four Branchmen, as well as twenty-five firemen, and gave his reasons:-

"My object in wishing a Sergeant appointed is that the men being now upon an equality with each other, it is quite impossible to get the whole of my instruction carried into effect, at a large fire, unless I have someone to rely upon to watch them carefully, and who will be considered in authority to do so, by his having more salary than the other men."

The branchmen, who actually handled the jets, Rose considered "run greater risks than those who work the engines only and get generally very much wet", and recommended the following pay scale:

Sergeant	£5-6-0 per annum
Branchmen	£4-6-0 per annum
Firemen	£3-9-0 per annum

It was finally decided to have 1 Superintendent, 1 Sergeant, 1 Messenger, 3 Corporals, 6 Branchmen

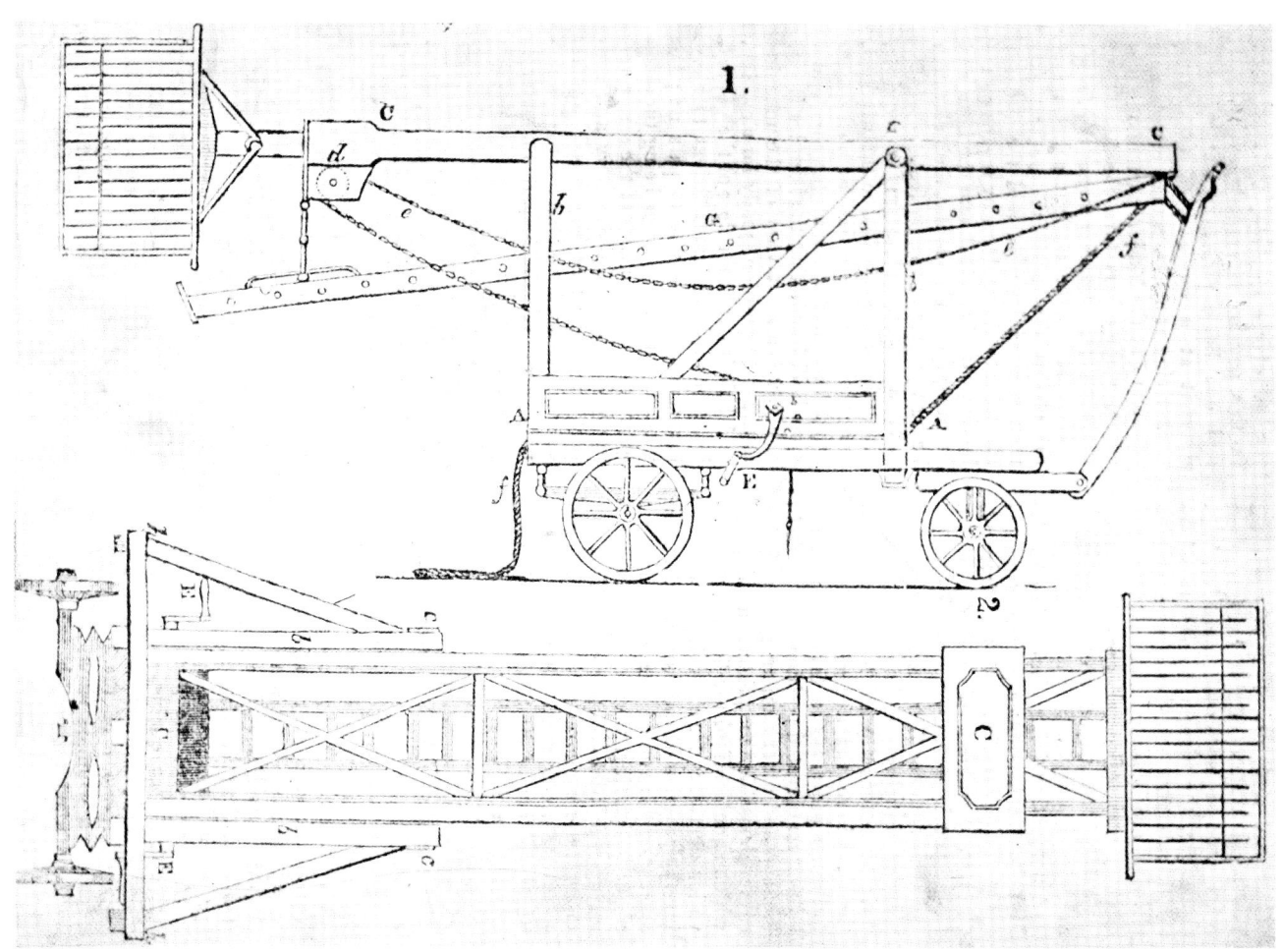

The 'Fireman's Elevator', Manchester's first fire escape, which was designed by Supt. William Rose

and 29 Lever Men (those who operated the levers of the engines).

William Rose's ability was proven in ways other than reorganising the Brigade. In 1830 he exhibited a fire escape, his own invention, to the Fire Engine Sub Committee. They were suitably impressed, as shown by a report to the Lamps etc Committee

> "<u>Reported</u> That we have minutely examined the machine above mentioned, we tried the pipes of the engine at various heights, and approve of its usefulness in case of fire for the purpose of a very superior access being obtained to the upper rooms and of conveying the water to the room on fire, and as an escape it is of the first consequence to save the lives of persons in danger, as such recommend that one of these machines be obtained for the use of the town."

It was not actually purchased until three years later when the Commissioners authorised £70 to be spent on the escape, generally known as the "Fireman's Elevator".

Despite his seemingly continual activity, there was not really enough work to occupy Superintendent Rose all of the time. At the end of 1830 the Committee decided that he should be additionally employed as an Assistant Office Clerk, and reside at the Police Yard. During the next decade, his duties were to increase even more when he became responsible for the Scavenging Department horses (1838) and was appointed Inspector of Lamps (1842). His loyalty and service to the Department were rewarded in 1834 when the Commissioners increased his salary from £150 to £200 per annum.

The improvements in the appliance fleet and discipline in the 1830's brought a new wave of public awareness of the Brigade, and glowing reports in the press regularly described the firemen's exploits to an eager readership.

From 1833 until 1843, the public of Manchester was treated to an annual exhibition of the Brigade's men and machinery, when the firemen joined in the annual May Day Stage Coach Procession through the town. This became a popular event, not only with the public, but also with the firemen, who traditionally ended the celebrations with a roast beef dinner, a plum pudding, (usually weighing about a hundred pounds) and a quantity of nut brown ale. It was also an opportunity for speech-making and mutual admiration; at the 1834 dinner, Superintendent Rose received a silver snuff-box, inscribed:-

> "Presented to Mr. William Rose by a few friends as a testimony of respect, and their admiration of the efficient state to which the Manchester Fire Engine Establishment has been brought by his energy and abilities 1st May 1834."

But it was not all pomp. The Brigade's good name had been earned by its fireground record. On the occasion of a fire at Wood's piano shop, Deansgate, in 1833, a customer at the adjacent Star Inn was heard to say that if this had been Liverpool, then the Star would most probably have burnt down.

A disastrous fire in August 1838 destroyed a waterproof cloth factory and resulted in the death of a Manchester fireman. On the Brigade's arrival the seven storey building, Messrs. Macintosh in Cambridge Street, was seriously involved, but nevertheless Superintendent Rose led his men to the fifth floor where they remained to fight the blaze despite the exploding of a 1000lb. solvent tank on the same floor. Two hours after the first call, the factory engineer started up machinery with the intention of working a pump to assist the firemen, but ironically his attempts had the opposite effect. In starting up he had forgotten to disconnect the gearing which turned the line-shafting, by now distorted due to the heat; as the twisted shafting turned the building began to shake. The resulting collapse caused the loss of four lives, one a fireman. As the vibrations were felt by the crews on the upper floors, one fireman was heard to shout "Oh James, it is like to be all up with us", and then ran out of the room to safety. A falling beam then struck Firemen James Watson and Henry Pollitt, who were only inches apart, operating a jet.

"Watson, as he was falling seized Pollitt's coat skirt, but the beam separated them; otherwise Pollitt must have shared Watson's fate. Pollitt then either fell or jumped through the chasm upon the floor below and became insensible; some portion of the falling floor and machinery came upon him and his right arm and leg were much crushed and his body strained and shaken by the rubbish. When he recovered he found himself in the situation described; and he had no doubt that Watson not being able to recover himself had fallen through the chasm in the floors to the bottom."

The body of the unfortunate Watson was recovered the next morning.

Superintendent Rose had another lucky escape at this fire, one of many in his illustrious career. As he was running out of the collapsing building, he was grabbed so furiously by Mr. Fletcher, the factory foreman, that he fell on his face and was covered in debris. He had just managed to smash a window with his fist to obtain some relief from the choking dust and flames, when another evacuee stood on his head. "For God's sake keep off my head" shouted Rose, (at least that is the recorded version!). In a short time he had extricated himself, suffering only contusions and cuts.

Three important advancements in the 1830's brought great improvements in the Brigade's turnout arrangements, and consequently its efficiency. In 1836, at William Rose's suggestion, five of the Town's Yard staff were trained as firemen so as to provide a crew of "at least seven" available for immediate turnout. In addition, Fireman Nathaniel Booth was appointed permanently to maintain the engines. The second development came in 1838 when the Commissioners purchased the scavenging horses from a private contractor, and appointed William Rose in charge of them for another £100 per year. Previously, the Fire Engine Establishment had to pay £50 per annum to the contractor for the hire of just one horse, but would now be able to use the Commissioner's own horses, with obvious advantages.

The third improvement was again due to William Rose's initiative. Reporting to the Lamps, etc. Committee in 1839, he pointed out "a very serious defect" in the service, due to the absence of permanent night staff.

Rose's prediction of conflagration breaking out at night dramatically came true. A huge fire broke out on Thursday 5th March 1840, in narrow Palace Square, off Market Street. A subsequent enquiry instigated by the Manchester Assurance Company, who suffered serious losses in the fire, showed the "serious defects" that William Rose had outlined. The Police watchman on duty in the area first learned of the fire, about 5.30 am, and went round his beat to notify other watchmen, ringing a small bell ("according to the instructions"). He did not inform the fire brigade though, admitting that he "did not know where the fire engines were kept, nor where the Police Yard was". It was also revealed that the fire was actually first perceived around 2 am by a private watchman, but that the Fire Brigade was not alerted until about 5.30 am, by another private watchman.

Superintendent Rose and Fireman Booth turned out straight away, reaching the scene in ten minutes. On arrival, they found that the police had not called the watermen and the mains were therefore dry. Whilst a man was being despatched to do this the Niagara was set to work using the water barrel. But there was a shortage of assistants; and so without further ado Rose went down to Market Street to "offer reward to those who would come forward".

After two hours hard fire-fighting, using five engines, the fire was surrounded. Two warehouses had been destroyed, and other buildings affected, but a large amount of property was saved, and the Manchester firemen were greatly praised. The enquiry concluded that any fault lay with the night policing system, and not with the Fire Brigade. Eventually a night fire staff of six men was instituted, in 1841.

In 1843, control of the Brigade passed to the Watch Committee of the new Borough Council. Other developments included a district station at Pollard Street, Ancoats, and new blue uniforms with, for the first time, fire helmets.

There were a number of large fires in the 1840's and 1850's. One of the most serious being on 2nd March 1844, involving a large pile of warehouses in George Street. Superintendent Rose turned out with his son Thomas (who regularly gave assistance albeit unpaid) on board the *Niagara* engine. Within a short space of time, the rest of the fleet had to be mustered, including the *Thetis* from Pollard Street, and one engine from Salford Fire Brigade. Fanned by a strong breeze, the fire spread from its point of origin, Messrs. Bryan's warehouse, to finally envelop the whole seven-storey block, which was about 150ft. x 100ft. and contained well over a dozen different occupiers. A shortage of pumping assistants was countered by sending for the soldiers of the 32nd from Tib Street Barracks who also helped control the crowds. The loss from this blaze amounted to £140,000.

Two months later, the two hundred seat Theatre Royal in Fountain Street was destroyed in less than one hour, and in August a £20,000 fire ravaged a comparatively new building in The Parsonage. William Rose felt obliged to resign in 1846 after winning a tender to supply horses to the Corporation. This meant he could no longer devote the whole of his time to the service, as was required. It would, however, ensure that horses were always readily available for the engines.

THE BURNING OF THE THEATRE ROYAL, FOUNTAIN STREET, MANCHESTER, 7TH MAY, 1844

One of the last things Rose did before resigning was to come almost to blows on the fireground with the Superintendent of the Salford Fire Police. The incident, on August 19th, was at Swinburn's provision shop on the Manchester side of Victoria Bridge. Two machines were turned out, with Rose in charge, and they arrived just before the Salford engine under Supt. Darling. The Manchester pumps were brought into action and soon had the fire under control, without recourse to using a third ordered on as a precaution. Darling's crew took a full twenty minutes to prepare their engine for action and after this time Rose politely informed him they were not required as the fire was out. The Salford Superintendent questioned Rose's judgement and on the latter's suggestion went upstairs to find some Manchester firemen engaged in damping-down operations. Nevertheless, he returned to the street and ordered his crew to direct a jet into the same room.

"I again demanded of him to desist", reported Rose, "when some angry words took place between us, and which might have led to a serious outbreak between the forces".

Following this the Watch Committee resolved, at Rose's request, not to allow the MFB to attend fires in Salford unless sent for by the authorities of that town, and to request the Salford Watch Committee to enforce a similar regulation. The first part of the resolution was in fact altered the following March so that the MFB could attend Salford but, unless first there, must wait until asked before taking any action. The second part, whereby Salford were asked not to attend uninvited, remained as "the Manchester Fire Brigade has been hitherto found sufficient for all emergencies".

Two monuments to William Rose's memory ensured that the citizens of Manchester remembered him for a long time. The first was "The Rose Light" (a splendid and decorative new gas lamp), erected in St. Ann's Square, which was lit on 1st May 1843, and named in recognition of his services to the Lamps Department. The second was a stained glass window in the Cathedral, representing Raphael's "Ascension", and installed in 1884 by Thomas to the memory of his father after his death nine years earlier.

Soon after the Victoria Bridge dispute of 1846 William Rose was succeeded by his son Thomas.

The new Superintendent soon became as well-loved and respected a character as his father had been while in office. If William was the courageous, progressive Chief Officer who had guided the MFB out of the depths of amateurism, then Thomas was the tall, handsome hero of the fireground who captured the hearts of Mancunians.

During Thomas Rose's first twelve months in office, a number of new types of equipment were considered, including a hose reel and two types of wheeled escape.

One of the escapes, Abraham Wivell's 'Improved National Fire Escape', made in Birmingham, was purchased for £65 in April, following a demonstration in the presence of the Mayor in Mosley Street. It was one of the earliest escapes in Britain and Manchester's first, apart from William Rose's Elevator. The apparatus could reach a height of fifty-five feet with main and upper ladders, had a 16 foot "single or first storey ladder", and was fitted with a canvas chute underneath for persons to slide down. In addition a separate jumping-sheet was carried.

The first test of the new Superintendent's command at a large fire came on the night of 11th August 1847, almost exactly a year from his official appointment. A huge fire destroyed a large block of buildings in the Pool Street area off Market Street, where the Arndale Centre now stands. At about 7.30 pm, Mrs. Wyndham (an actress) and a Mrs. Sloan were sitting in the Old Swan Hotel in Pool Street when they saw smoke and flames in a window of Frederick Smith, paper dealer, directly opposite. Mrs. Sloan ran into the street shouting "fire" but nobody else could see it at the time. Henry Hewitt, a tailor in the premises next door to the Hotel, saw the same thing soon afterwards and also ran down to the street. But the spread of fire was now so rapid that as he arrived in the street he was just in time to see flames jumping the nine-foot Pool Street to his own premises. Thomas Rose received the first call at 7.50 pm and was "on the spot with the Thames Engine and a Company of firemen" in five minutes. He was met with the sight of flames issuing from every window along the Pool Street side and from two floors on the Market Street face of the building, as well as from Hewitt's and other premises across Pool Street. Within an incredibly short space of time, flames appeared in New Brown Street, at the rear of the block, whilst the fire was spreading southwards from Hewitt's towards Cunliffe and Brook's bank and the Old Swan. Brands were flying over Shudehill and Victoria Station. Supt. Rose ordered jets to be laid from the high-pressure main along Market Street, but the plugs were jammed due to the pressure, delaying operations by some five minutes, a long time when a fire is spreading. Thomas, assisted by his father who was now, of course, a civilian, but keen to volunteer in the Rose tradition, realised that the only hope now was to prevent the blaze spreading to crowded and as yet unaffected property around the fire.

But the efforts of eight Manchester engines were not sufficient to contain the fire and Rose had to send for assistance from Salford. He had obviously tried to manage without their help in view of the rather delicate arrangements between the two brigades at this time, and Superintendent Darling, in his annual report the following month, gloated that he had been poised "fully three quarters of an hour waiting for a message from the Manchester Superintendent". Soon after the arrival of the *Nile* and *Deluge* engines from Salford, Rose needed still further reinforcements. After consultation with the Mayor and the Chief Constable, it was decided to send messengers to Stockport and Bolton for help. However, by ten o'clock the fire was under control, and messengers were again despatched to halt them. After ten hours hard firefighting with twelve jets the fire was finally extinguished, having caused £35,000 worth of damage. The expenses incurred by the Brigade, including paying 4/- a man to 494 casual assistants, totalled £166.

The main reasons for the extremely rapid spread of this fire were the congested buildings and the high exposure hazard of narrow streets; but another important reason was the actual design of the warehouse block in which it commenced. Manchester textile warehouses of this period were invariably of the same style of construction: large light wells in the centre, combustible timber staircases and the walls lined with wood to prevent damage to the plaster when handling goods. They therefore had everything a fire needed to develop quickly, and this was frequently proved. A London architect, Mr. Tite FRS, once commented, "if I was called upon as an architect to construct a building which would be capable of burning down in the quickest and most effective manner, I would adopt the very principle of the Manchester warehouses".

Three years after the Market Street blaze another serious warehouse fire broke out in the town centre. Shortly before midnight on Thursday 21st March 1850, a policeman spotted a fire on the third floor of J.P. and G. Westhead & Co., a smallware dealers, in Piccadilly. He immediately hailed a passing cab to take him to the Town's Yard, but by the time he arrived, the fire had assumed such serious proportions that another officer near the Yard could see a glow in the sky and was already alerting the firemen living nearby. The *Thames* engine was in attendance at 12.12 am, under Senior Corporal George Dearden, Thomas Rose being away. A further eight engines from Manchester, and two from Salford, using good water supplies including the Infirmary pond, could do nothing to contain the fire which raged through the building for four hours and caused a massive £100,000 worth of damage. Burnt materials from the warehouse were reputedly found in Levenshulme, over three miles away. The following day, Firemen James Naylor and Charles McGarry were at work on the Back Piccadilly side of the building when a wall collapsed on them. Naylor was extricated in ten minutes, seriously injured, but alive. McGarry was located soon afterwards and taken to the Infirmary, just opposite, were he was found to be dead. Unfortunately, Naylor too died one month later.

Of course there is often a lighter side to the many serious fires which have raged in the city throughout its history. When All Saints Church was destroyed in February 1850 two weddings scheduled for the morning after the fire had to be cancelled. One couple proceeded instead to the Cathedral but the second pair were unwilling to make other arrangements. Therefore, standing amongst the debris and charred timbers, and surrounded by the begrimed firemen, the happy couple were united by the Rev. Garrett!

In the same year a new development took place which was of tremendous importance to the Brigade. A high-pressure, constant-supply water system began to flow from new reservoirs in the Longdendale Valley, to the east of Manchester. The scheme, the result of two years' work from the passing of the relevant legislation, was completed

Fire at All Saints Church, 1850.

finally in 1853. So great was the improvement that the use of the engines (and assistants) dwindled due to increased mains pressure, and the fire loss statistics showed a dramatic fall.

Simultaneous with the opening of the new supply was the installation of 'fire cocks', or hydrants. These were, at the time, an unbelievable improvement over the old fire plugs which had been the cause of many a soaked fireman when the wooden plug was removed and the standpipe driven in.

The high-pressure supply and hydrants were really christened on the night of 1st March 1854, when a devastating fire broke out in the town centre. The blaze was in a range of warehouses occupied chiefly by Messrs. J. Rylands & Sons, fustian and linen manufacturers, in Bread Street, off High Street. All ten Manchester appliances plus four others were in attendance, but thanks to the now excellent water mains only four were actually used. Fourteen hydrants were pressed into service to supply an impressive 3000 gallons per minute through nineteen jets. This was in marked contrast to the fire seven years earlier in Market Street, a matter of yards away, when nearly as many engines attended but were all pumping furiously at the hands of over 500 men. The Rylands fire broke out in the centre block of three buildings around 10.00 pm and was soon discovered. There were several employees still on the premises who wasted time by removing the ledgers, and no doubt themselves, to the safety of the nearby Angel Inn. Thus the fire spread and leapt narrow Bread Street and New High Street before the very eyes of Thomas Rose. Before turning out, he had ordered on the rest of the appliances and the remainder of his men as a precaution. In fact, forty-seven of the establishment were in attendance at the fire, three being on leave. The fire drove on towards High Street, where it was stopped by a wall of water manipulated by a 25-strong crew of firemen. Around midnight two mounted troops of the 1st Royal Dragoons arrived from Hulme Barracks to control the vast crowd, many of whom were anxious to help. The fight lasted throughout that Wednesday night until almost 8.00 am when the crews were reduced and the fire burned out. The damage totalled over £100,000.

There was no provision for attending over-the-border incidents at this period - powers were only extended from the old Township of Manchester area to the whole Borough in 1849 - but occasionally attendances were made. Usually it was a serious incident which resulted in the MFB being called, but in January 1854 two engines and men travelled third class by a special train to Ashton-under-Lyne to deal with a relatively minor blowing-room fire. The railway expenses totalled £8 1s 0d. In June of the same year the *Thames* and *Water Witch* responded to a serious mill fire in Worsley, passing the Salford contingent of two engines en route. The seven-mile journey was covered in 34 minutes from time of call, and two more machines followed on. The *Guardian* remarked in its following edition that "the saving of property through the prompt arrival of the Manchester engines was very great. This is an instance of the good results of always having men on duty in the yard, with engines and horses ready".

A serious problem at this time was the high number of injuries which occurred on the fireground. Rose was concerned that there was no provision for official medical attendance and petitioned the Watch Committee. The matter was resolved in May 1856 when Mr. McKeand was appointed Brigade Surgeon. Of greater importance, though, was the saving of life at fires. From about 1856, pressures from various directions were applied to the Watch Committee to provide more effective means of rescuing persons trapped in blazing buildings. In January of that year, inhabitants in the central area of the City asked for a fire escape to be provided either in Piccadilly or St. Ann's Square.

The Piccadilly and Market Street area was a particularly high fire and life risk, containing not

Demonstration of a new escape in Albert Square, 1849. Bought at a cost of £65, the main ladder was 32 ft. and the upper ladder, 20 ft. A length of canvas surrounded by a copper mesh acted as a chute for persons to slide to safety.

only the Infirmary but several hotels and large commercial properties. The buildings were congested and the streets narrow; when the opportunity to rebuild sensibly had arisen it was often missed. After the 1854 Ryland's fire, for example, it was reported that the premises were "rebuilt with the same confined passages surrounding it - they are not worthy the names of streets - which existed before the fire".

There was little progress in the provision of an escape for the next two or three years. A couple of dramatic rescues reflecting on the Brigade's poor arrangements apparently did nothing to hurry the situation. On June 3rd 1858 a fire in a shop on Deansgate in the small hours trapped three women, two men and a child on the second floor. Although Rose turned the escape out on the initial call knowing that persons were trapped, all six were rescued by police and civilians before its arrival, a ladder having been balanced on the shoulders of a man named Hayes, to enable it to reach the window. Whether the crews, who rarely used the apparatus, or the escape itself, badly maintained and several years old, would have been up to carrying out an effective rescue even were they on time is a matter for speculation. The second fire, in broad daylight, occurred at a three-storey multi-occupied house in Edge Street in February 1859. Once again, persons were trapped on an upper floor, this time a woman and three children. Two of the children were thrown down to safety and the woman and other child were eventually rescued by passers-by who tied two ladders together. The escape was not even taken to this fire.

After an incident in November 1859 when a twelve-year-old boy died, Rose again requested siting the escape in Piccadilly, and repeated his proposal of using beat policemen to operate it when required. The Watch Committee finally acceded. A new escape was ordered from William Rose in January 1860 at a cost of £45 and the following December, after another long years' wait, the Committee gave approval to its siting in front of the Infirmary. Also approved was the payment of 2d per journey per man to "A" Division policemen - who were to be trained by Superintendent Rose - for moving it to and from the Police Yard every day. It had taken just under five years to attain an escape station in the City centre, and this was still only a night-time arrangement.

Meanwhile, interest in means of escape was continuing, with unfortunate consequences on one occasion. On October 19th 1860, Senior Corporal Dearden, who had served 22 years in the Brigade, was demonstrating a sheet fire escape he had made, in Mosley Street, when he fell to the ground ten feet below. Shaken, he immediately went home but sadly died from his injuries three days later.

A serious fire in June 1861 proved to be the last of many in Thomas Rose's fifteen year career. On the evening of the fifteenth, the whole Brigade was turned out to Messrs. Parr, Curtis and Madeley's machine works in Chapel Street, Ancoats. Rose arrived in twelve minutes with the *Thames*, and found the Pollard Street crew with two jets already at work, as flames belched out of the joiners' shops and threatened the main mill. The men struggled to obtain water from hydrants and the Ashton-Under-Lyne Canal in intolerable conditions. As the strong east wind blew the flames inevitably across the narrow yard to the main block, spalling stonework showered around the men. A mile and a half of hose was laid through what Rose described as "one of the densest and most unmanageable crowds" he had ever seen, some of whom pulled the hose and damaged standpipes. Others threw iron and furniture out of the building, laming three firemen. Only the previous night one fireman had been killed and three injured in a fire at a Rubber Works in Ardwick.

The Watch Committee ordered an immediate inquiry into both the fire and the Brigade's efficiency. One month later Superintendent Rose resigned to become the Manchester agent of the Royal Exchange Insurance Company.

Chapter Four

REORGANISATION

"The fire brigade is maintained by the local ratepayers for the benefit of the city of Manchester and not all the world beyond."

Ald. BENNETT
Council meeting 3rd July 1872.

The Watch Committee enquiry was postponed until a new Superintendent was found, which was not until February 1862 when Alfred Tozer of the London Fire Engine Establishment was appointed.

Tozer's credentials were impeccable. His father was a Hand-in-Hand Insurance Company fireman, and before he was twenty years old, Alfred had joined him in his work. In December 1853 he had saved two lives and was awarded the silver medal of the Royal Society for the Protection of Life from Fire - the first London fireman to be so decorated. Two years later, during the Crimean war, he took charge of the firefighting arrangements in the base camps and hospitals, notably the famous Scutari Hospital where he served with Florence Nightingale. On his return to London he served at Watling Street fire station and was confidential clerk to the legendary James Braidwood; he had attended the disastrous Tooley Street fire which had resulted in the death of Braidwood.

Within twelve months of his appointment Tozer had transformed the Brigade beyond recognition.

One of his earliest innovations was the introduction of the portable handpump (or "Tozer pump", as the device became almost universally known), which enabled firemen to attack minor fires without inflicting the water damage which was so prevalent when using large jets. But this was only the beginning.

He soon produced a master plan which was to provide a greater distribution of appliances and a more efficient use of personnel. His recommendations included:-

a) increasing the permanent staff from 7 to 27
b) disposing of all engines except the *Thames*
c) purchasing five new manuals "of the newest and best construction"
d) setting up five more street escape stations manned day and night
e) providing first-aid fire equipment at twelve police stations around the City
f) erecting a new headquarters station with accommodation for 16 men and horses
g) rebuilding the Pollard Street station

On 7th January 1863 the Council agreed to the reorganisation plan in total, and one week later three new escapes were on the run! Before the end of the month an assistant superintendent (James Davies), two engineers and 11 branchmen had been appointed.

During the summer the first of the five new

manual pumps were supplied - one each from William Rose of Salford and Shand, Mason & Co. of London. Despite being of the latest design they must nevertheless have been overshadowed by an appliance demonstrated a few weeks later in the Town's Yard. In July, the famous Crystal Palace steam fire engine trials had taken place in London, and on 4th August Manchester saw its first steamer when the American appliance "Victoria", made appropriately in Manchester, New Hampshire, was shown to civic dignitaries. The results were "astonishing", up to eight jets being supplied from the three-ton machine and the performance was repeated before a cheering public the following day. It appeared likely said the media that manual pumps would now be phased out altogether, but this was not to be. The offer of William Rose (who had arranged the exhibition) to loan the steamer to the Brigade for a period was apparently declined and a week later three new manuals were ordered.

Although Manchester had no desires to become steam pioneers, important progress was still being made and at three minutes past seven on the morning of 1st November 1863 the first call was sent via the new "Universal" telegraph system which linked all stations by means of signalling apparatus.

With developments such as these finance became an important consideration. In twelve months the Brigade's annual estimate had leapt from £1600 to £4000. The Watch Committee felt that the previous insurance contributions of about £100 per annum were not enough considering the Brigade's improved efficiency. Accordingly the offices were approached for a joint contribution of £2500 towards the maintenance of the Brigade. At a meeting of insurance companies in London in November 1863 the whole principle of payment towards *any* fire brigade was condemned, but consent was given to an experimental payment of £1750 per annum for two years, backdated to March. The deal, agreed to by the Corporation, guaranteed contributing offices exemption from all ordinary expenses for the attendance of the Brigade at fires, up to 72 hours watching duties by firemen after a fire and the right to reconsider the amount paid.

Not every premise was covered by insurance though, and a scale of charges for attendance at the many uninsured properties was agreed on in March 1864.

In the summer the services of the last 'occasional men' were dispensed with, making Manchester the first permanently-employed fire brigade in Britain. The Chief Constable's annual report for the year ending 29th September 1864 revealed that a record number of fire calls (226) had been answered, coupled with a record *low* fire loss figure of £20,540. This remarkable achievement was, stated the report, "clearly due to the distribution of the Brigade throughout the City, and

Supt. Alfred Tozer (1862-1892).

to the introduction of telegraphic communication."

Work on the two large fire stations was progressing and in August 1865 staff moved from the inadequate accommodation at Pollard Street yard to purpose-built premises in Boond Street (still referred to ever since as "Pollard Street"), a few blocks away. The new "chief station" in Jacksons Row was completed in January 1866. The facilities were an immeasurable improvement over those at Clarence Street yard, and it was to be the Brigade's headquarters for forty years.

Faced with another period of high expenditure the Council predictably looked towards the insurance offices for an increased contribution, and a new rate £2,000 per annum for two years was agreed, the companies still being opposed to the idea of contributing at all to the Brigade. The Watch Committee, no doubt bearing in mind the apparent shakiness of the arrangement sought further powers to make charges beyond those granted under the 1844 Police Act. The result was Section 20 of the Manchester Town Hall and Improvement Act 1866, which laid down that for every fire which broke out in the City, the owners of property endangered were liable to pay not only the actual Brigade expenses but also a "reasonable charge for the expenses incurred by the establishment and maintenance of the fire brigade". In case of dispute, the justices were to decide and enforce payment. In September, the Council agreed to a charging system based upon property value in which there were minimum and maximum charges; no person was to pay more than the total value of his property. Of course the system would still only be used in cases where the insurance contribution scheme was not applicable (eg. uninsured property).

Steady progress continued to be made in the Brigade. In April 1867 the infirmary escape was

Horse-drawn manual pump and personnel at Town Yard, shortly before its closure in 1866.

37

manned by firemen for the first time - a small move which rapidly paid for itself in terms of fire losses. In March 1870 the Brigade purchased its first horses, so ending the long-standing arrangement with William Rose and in October Superintendent Tozer wore a new type of smoke-respirator at a mill fire, probably the first use of breathing-apparatus in Manchester.

Water supplies at fires were still a problem, despite the completion of the Longdendale scheme some twenty years previously. The older areas of the City where the mains were particularly inadequate suffered most. In December 1869 a petition called for improved supplies in the Hulme area. The problem was highlighted in December 1870 when a £20,000 fire destroyed Reilly's cabinet works in Barrack Street, Hulme. The Brigade was obliged to pump from local swimming baths as the 3- and 4-inch mains were practically useless, and it transpired that the waterworks foreman had not turned on the Godley pressure for fear of breaking the main! A Waterworks Sub-Committee inquiry into the fire concluded that the Brigade should accept whatever pressure there was and use their engines from the outset. This was in sharp contrast to the claims, twenty years earlier, that the new high-pressure supply was so good that fire engines would be superfluous.

Clearly the water problem was not to be solved overnight, but Tozer was convinced after the Reilly's fire that the time had now come to buy Manchester's first steam fire engine. The Fire Brigade Sub-Committee agreed unanimously and on 5th January 1871 a Merryweather "medium class" steamer was put through its paces in Albert Square. After a second test in Water Street two days later with even better results it was agreed that a similar machine be purchased for £600. The demonstration model was allowed to remain in the City until the new one was delivered "in case of a serious outbreak".

Boond Street (Pollard Street) Fire Station, photographed May 1906.

Its chance to prove itself "in anger" came on February 4th when fire swept through Shaw, Jardine and Co.'s spinning mill in Butler Street, the largest fire for five years. A huge crowd, "literally mad with excitement", stood on the hose, causing it to burst and police reinforcements were required to disperse the mob. Whether the object of their frenzied attention was the fire or the new-fangled fire engine may never be known. The steamer was set to work from the Rochdale Canal and gave a good account of itself. It was later calculated that the total expense of operating the steamer at this fire was about 3% of that of a manual due to the saving in manpower. In addition, its output was many times greater.

The Brigade's own steamer was delivered on 18th June and publicly tested on 22nd in Albert Square. Two days later it saw real action at another Ancoats mill fire, much larger than the Shaw, Jardine's incident. This time the premises were McConnell's mill in Union Street. Four separate outstations received calls for the blaze at 7.20 pm and Tozer turned out the whole force immediately. On arrival the three top floors of the eight-storey, 300 ft. long mill were well alight and two miles of hose were laid to twenty jets in a very short time. Using the new steamer, the fire was stopped, incredibly, in three hours.

The period up to the turn of the century seemed fraught with disputes over charges and attendances. After another disagreement with the combined insurance offices over contributions, the Corporation considered over-the-border incidents. In June 1872 a call was received by telegram for a serious

Chief Fire Station, Jackson's Row, opened 1866.

factory fire in Warrington. The Brigade was only prevented from attending by the bungling of the railway company who would not lay on a special train after hours to transport the firemen, without permission from London. As a result of incidents like these, the Watch Committee reviewed the whole question and resolved in December not to attend *any* call beyond the City boundary unless the appropriate local authority had made (financial) arrangements with the Council.

The decision took the small local townships by surprise as most relied on the City for their protection. Rusholme and Moss Side promptly formed their own volunteer brigades; Gorton considered one but adjourned the matter. The Crumpsall Local Board were not really concerned as their own volunteer brigade was just becoming established. Its appliances comprised of a Rose manual pump and a horse cart, horses being supplied by the Manchester Carriage Company. The Rusholme and Moss Side Brigades were more modest affairs, each having only a small hose cart and a few men, and most districts remained unprotected throughout most of 1873.

A fire in Newton Heath in November 1873 forced the Committee to reconsider its attitude. The building involved, William Holland's Victoria Mill, was, in fact, only 600 yards beyond the City boundary in Lower Vickers Street. Shortly before 6 am the Goulden Street and Pollard Street stations each received a call for the mill, the top floor of which was alight. In accordance with the General Orders, both stations refused assistance. Mr. Tozer did, however, inform the Salford and Broughton brigades and sent a Manchester waterman to assist. By now the top three floors were involved and a further call to Headquarters at 6.25 am reported persons trapped. In spite of orders the Goulden Street and Pollard Street escapes were immediately turned out, with a crew of ten, and Superintendent Tozer also responded. On arrival one woman was rescued by escape, but no further assistance was rendered, Superintendent Tozer merely advising the brigades present, which now included Crumpsall and a local works outfit.

Predictably, there were swift demands for an end to the ban, but the Corporation was, it stated, "not by any means anxious to send their brigade into the outdistricts". The districts, it was felt, should provide their own fire cover. Operating their own fire services was out of the question for most of them, and it was clear that they would either have to accede to the City's demands for financial contributions or be without protection. Negotiations dragged on until the summer of 1875 when the Council settled for a total income of £525 from eight townships in return for fire cover, provided the combined offices paid equal amounts. The eight areas to be covered were Bradford, Crumpsall, Gorton, Moss Side, Newton Heath, Openshaw, Rusholme and Stretford. Over the next few years the various district authorities gradually joined in the scheme until most of the surrounding areas were covered by the MFB.

The Brigade had become extremely professional under Tozer's command. His remarkable insight into firefighting is reflected in his introduction to the men of some of the basic operational techniques still in use today. He was a firm believer in fighting fires from *inside* a building, which was already a Manchester tradition, though not without its dangers.

Tozer's rules and frequently-issued "General Orders" covered every aspect of the job and discipline was his strong point. The innovations introduced by Alfred Tozer are too numerous to list, but range from such things as steamers and quick-acting stable doors to standard messages and the carrying of salvage sheets on appliances. His reputation as an authority on firefighting and brigade management was renowned and he was frequently called on for advice. But behind the cool professional was a very human person who was as much

right: Supt. Tozer with the Brigade's first steam fire engine, 1871.

THE JUNCTION, HULME: A CALL TO FIRE (UPPER JACKSON STREET SCHOOL IN THE BACKGROUND).

remembered for his love of animals as his firefighting. He was a great writer, not only about the fire service but also about natural history. His not infrequent contributions to various journals turned "Our Jim" and "Our Bruce" almost into legends. The former, a black and tan terrier, joined the Brigade in 1862 as a stray. He was allowed to run to fires with the engines and soon became known as the Manchester Fire Dog. He soon acquired a knack for knowing when a call was being received, especially at night, and (until his death in 1876) used to alert the men with his "firebark", usually before the bell was sounded. Bruce was the firemen's favourite horse, a grey purchased among the first eight of 1870. A former Manchester Carriage Company horse, he ended his days in the police patrol department under a Sergeant Bruce. He was best known for opening and closing his own stable door and helping himself to drinks from a wooden tap, or from the end of a hose, with which he was once said to have deliberately wet a troublesome fireman. He also used to perform tricks in the yard and amuse the firemen's children. On the occasion of his death in 1878, due to a stone weighing nearly six pounds in his bowels, Tozer arranged for the stone - the size of a bowls ball - to be displayed in a glass case at Jackson's Row. The case, suitably inscribed "In memory of 'Our Bruce,' " remained a Manchester Fire Brigade relic for many years.

The continued success of the reorganisation plan was shown by a number of dramatic escape rescues in the seventies. Unfortunately, despite the obvious

Goulden Street Station, New Cross, opened 1872. This building still stands today, directly opposite the new Thompson Street fire station.

advantages of escapes they frequently met trouble with overhead obstructions such as telephone wires, which were increasing in number. In his annual report for the year ending September 1880, Superintendent Tozer cited 19 cases of escapes colliding with telephone wires below 30 ft. After one incident in Bradford Road, when a telephone wire attached to a house chimney brought down the stack causing fatal injuries to a woman passer-by, the Post Office agreed to resite all low wires, either higher up or else underground.

The telephone was becoming extremely popular and by 1884 the Brigade had replaced its signal telegraphs, with a new telephone system of its own. Other developments at this time included the introduction of the Morris instantaneous coupling in 1882, the provision of ambulances at fire stations (1884) and the appointment of two permanent turncocks.

The insurance contribution scheme broke down yet again in March 1884, and, despite some diplomatic intervention by the Mayor, no settlement was forthcoming. The Corporation immediately imposed the percentage scale of charges - which the companies advised their clients to resist - and ultimately found themselves in court under the terms of the 1866 Act. In a test case in June 1885 the Stipendiary Magistrate, Mr. Headlam, reduced a charge of £73-10-0 (based on the percentage system) to £26-10-0, considering instead the time engaged by the Brigade. The percentage system was, he felt an unreasonable one and following his decision the scale was revised accordingly. A settlement was eventually reached with the offices and the contribution scheme was continued from 1886.

The 1866 Act was to lose some more of its bite when the City was extended in 1885. The relevant legislation concerning the taking over of Harpurhey,

New steamers on test prior to delivery to the MFB, c1886.

Bradford and Rusholme provided for extension of the provisions of all local acts *except* Section 20 of the Manchester Town Hall and Improvement Act 1866 (under which section fire brigade charges were levied). The effect was that no charge could be made for the Brigade's services in the new portions of the City, and this pattern was to be repeated for all subsequent boundary extensions. Thus, as the City became larger over the years, a greater percentage of its area was provided with a free fire service.

The Brigade was again redistributed to cover the new areas. Rusholme had a fire brigade of its own and it was agreed that, for a time, the services of the eight volunteers at Monmouth Street could be retained.

On 12th November 1885 they assisted at a £150,000 blaze in Portland Street which was accompanied by the thrilling rescue of a young man trapped on the top floor of the multi-occupancy warehouse whilst trying to fight the fire. To reach him, Engineer Hunt made his way to the roof of the building and, in dense smoke, crept along the cornice until he was directly above the youth. He then passed down a lifeline (with the assistance of a brave civilian who had joined him) which the man was able to grasp and so swing clear of the building. For several seconds he hung desperately over the crowded City street until he was carefully lowered on to the head of the Piccadilly escape, at which point he passed out. Two other firemen then brought him down to safety.

An incident in 1887 was probably the most destructive in Mr. Tozer's time. Just before noon on 22nd June a deafening explosion, heard for miles around, shook the Cornbrook district. The centre of the blast was the chemical works of Messrs. Roberts, Dale and Co. on Cornbrook Road, half of which was destroyed in the explosion. There was extensive damage to surrounding property, including the Pomona Gardens, site of the Jubilee Exhibition that year, and all that remained of the drying stove where the initial outbreak had occurred was an eight foot-deep crater. Two deaths occurred - one a workman caught in the blast, and the other small child suffering from shock and the effects of poisonous fumes. The Manchester firemen, helped by the Barracks Brigade and a Salford crew, took four hours to bring the blaze under control.

Further boundary extensions in November 1890 resulted in a rash of new premises. The most important of these were three new stations opened in 1892 at Harpurhey, Miles Platting and Chorlton-on-Medlock. There were also a number of escape and handpump stations in the new districts, but the most novel additions comprised twelve street boxes in the City centre and Chorlton-on-Medlock areas. These housed a "Tozer" pump and two buckets.

One result of the boundary extensions was the taking over of the Crumpsall Volunteer Fire Brigade and its station in Trees Street. The Brigade had continued to survive since its formation in 1872 having seen three captains and despite the resignation of all the firemen in 1881. This now meant that Moss Side was the only outdistrict with its own fire service.

Simultaneous with the new stations, two Merryweather medium-sized steamers were purchased to cover the new extensions, and together with an 1888 addition meant that a total of six steam appliances were now available at five of the residential stations.

These numerous additions to the Brigade were Alfred Tozer's last major contribution, as he retired in the summer of 1892. He had been a fireman for 41 years and after completing 30 years in Manchester was its longest-serving fire chief, a record never since equalled. He was genuinely reluctant to leave the Brigade, but now over sixty years of age and no longer enjoying the best of health, he felt unable to continue any longer. Mr. Tozer was a great loss to the Brigade, having done more to increase its professionalism and status than any, but Manchester could be proud to have enjoyed the service of the most notable member of Britain's most famous firefighting family. To succeed Mr. Tozer the Committee promoted John Lacey Savage.

At the time of Mr. Savage's appointment the Brigade was becoming more and more interested in fire prevention and the hazards which were responsible for outbreaks of fire. After a potentially serious fire involving a common lodging house in Newton Heath, it was found that 150 beds had been crammed into the upper floors of a former warehouse. Mr. Savage was asked to report on the number of buildings containing a sleeping risk above fifty feet - the limit of the Brigade's escapes. His report, completed in November, included the suggestion that the fly-ladder escapes should be converted to the telescopic principle so as not to foul overhead wires - still a problem.

There was clearly a need for increased ladder-power; several new warehouses were being erected in the City centre and, without exception, all were lofty structures. On 16th May 1894 a fire broke out in Messrs. Nordlinger's new five-storey building on the corner of Portland Street and Princess Street.

Mr. Savage and his men were on the spot five minutes after the evening call, with a steamer, manual, three tenders and the Piccadilly escape, recently converted to reach 66 ft., but the blaze

New Street Fire Station

Ash Street Fire Station

already involved two floors. On arrival Mr. Savage was informed of two missing persons at the rear, one being immediately found calling up the stairs to the other but without response. Jets were immediately brought to bear and, braving heat and dense smoke, a crew fought their way upstairs, only to find that the man was on the roof having opened a skylight. The new Shand Mason 80 ft. escape was sent for and, pending its arrival, the Piccadilly ladder was positioned to the roof, which happened to be 67 ft. 6 in. to the gutter!

Undaunted, Firemen William Lawrence and John Clayton ascended the ladder to carry out the most famous rescue in the history of the MFB. The head of the escape was just short, so Clayton formed himself into a "human ladder", with one hand on the escape and one against the wall, over which Lawrence climbed and managed to drag himself onto the roof. The return journey was even more breathtaking. After pulling the dazed man from the skylight down which he was about to fall, Lawrence then lowered him bodily over the gutter to the waiting Clayton. Somehow the victim was manoeuvred onto the escape and the trio made their perilous way down. While this incredible scene was being enacted, Mr. Savage had managed to silence the vast crowd, but as soon as the rescue party reached the street, "a thrilling cheer rent the air, the like of which has probably never been heard in Manchester". The Superintendent, in commending the actions of Clayton and Lawrence, remarked that he could not recall a "more striking case of courage and ability". He was also loud in his praise of the crews who had so ably confined the fire to the original building which was built, amazingly, on the site of Engineer Hunt's thrilling fire rescue of 1885. As well as receiving the Watch Committee's new Silver Medal for Bravery, the two rescuers were each awarded the Silver Medal of the Quiver Heroes Fund - inaugurated by a London periodical of that name - this latter

Lacey Savage, Chief Officer, 1892-1899.

Steam fire engine at work at the Cornbrook explosion, 1887.

ceremony being performed publicly by the Lord Mayor.

William Lawrence was one of the Brigade's most colourful characters. Born Samuel Mills, he ran away to sea at the age of thirteen, taking his new name from a passer-by who agreed to sign his enlistment form.

Most Manchester firemen of this period were ex-sailors, and Savage firmly believed they were the best men for the job.

"They require no teaching in making lines fast, in hanging on by their eyebrows, as it were, in doing without the regulation hours of sleep, in having the faculty to turn out thoroughly keen and wide awake at any moment night or day, and for their general handiness", he once said, "they understand discipline without losing independence, that is to say they will obey orders but in an emergency they can use their mother wit and come out of the ordeal creditably". "They are a bit difficult to manage at first", he added, "but they soon settle down".

The firemen brought many naval practices and expressions with them, which soon became part of MFB tradition. At funerals, for instance, Manchester firemen always wore their black silk scarves around the left arm, which was said to date back to Nelson's time. Words such as "smoko", meaning a tea break (not peculiar to Manchester), and "Paddy Wester" meaning a fireman sent temporarily from another station, or an outsider, can still be heard on City fire stations today. The latter expression is thought to have derived from a Liverpool lodging house of the same name used by seamen and from whence casual labour could usually be obtained.

At this time, and since 1886, all new recruits were "sworn in" as police constables, whilst the Superintendent had been directly responsible to the Chief Constable since Thomas Rose's day. Neither were, of course, called upon to do any normal police

47

duties. Mr. Savage was not in favour, and indeed was rapped for speaking against the system soon after his appointment in 1893. The close relationship between the two services was becoming less relevant, and if anything, it was more useful to the police than the Fire Brigade. The latter, with its 27 horses constantly available was a very convenient source of horsepower for the ambulance and prison van services, though to the detriment of the Brigade. Mr. Savage was convinced that an efficient Brigade should not share its horses with any other service and backed up his complaint with a vetinary surgeon's report on the unsuitability of attaching prison vans to quality fire brigade horses. The point was taken by the Watch Committee and alternative arrangements were promised for both ambulance and prison vans.

Only one hurdle now remained and, no doubt to Mr. Savage's delight, it was decided to cease the "swearing in" of firemen from March 1898 and the Brigade was able to go its own way without any responsibility to the Chief Constable. Thus in a short space of time, Mr. Savage had rid the Brigade of all the encumbrances associated with police control and it must have been with some sense of achievement that he submitted his resignation in 1898 after 25 years service. Defective eyesight, caused through injury at a fire, had plagued him for some time and he now felt he would be a danger to his men. Savage was not the type to give up easily - once, after breaking his leg on the fireground, he worked for a further three hours without noticing - but now felt obliged to finish, a year before his time was due. Perhaps he had struggled on for so long to realise his ambitions of a Fire Brigade free from police influence.

In seven short years Mr. Savage had made his own indelible mark on the Brigade and brought about some not insignificant changes which would prepare the Brigade fittingly for the twentieth century.

Unknown Escape Station.

above: Firemen's children Pollard Street.
below: Personnel at Pollard Street 1894.
opposite: Firemen's Arch commemorating the opening of the Manchester Ship Canal 1894.

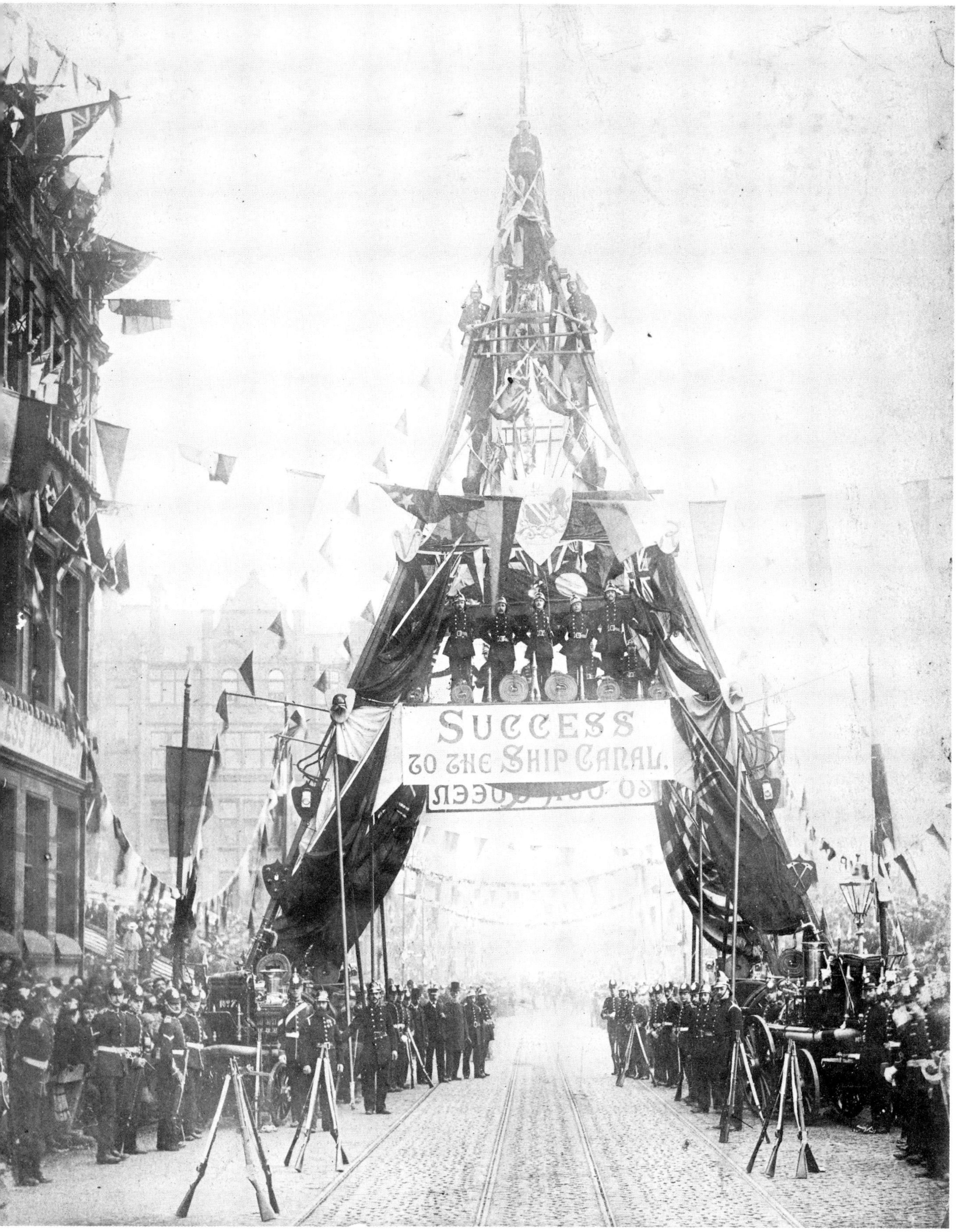
SUCCESS
TO THE SHIP CANAL.

Chapter Five

THE NEW HEADQUARTERS

"The fire brigade of a great city should be directed not by a Chief Constable but by an expert fireman, untrammelled by any other professional occupation."

THE MANCHESTER FIRE BRIGADE
Hubbard & Williams 1898

Life in the MFB at the turn of the century was hard and monotonous. The men worked long hours on the "continuous duty" system, with only one day off in every thirteen, their families usually leading drab lives in one of the residential stations.

The only relief the men were permitted on their long twelve day tours of duty was the unofficial practice of "going to the corner" - a quick drink at the local hostelry - and they were disciplined if they took too long over this. For men on street-escape duty, conditions were worse; working in pairs on 8.00 'til 8.00 shifts the men still had routine work and fire calls to deal with when they returned to their home station. If it was one man's leave day, his partner had to provide total cover until he returned.

The Brigade was still feeling its feet as a Department in its own right since its separation form the Police in 1898. In February 1899 the Watch Committee advertised for a "Chief Officer" who was to be under forty-five years of age and have experience of city firefighting. The successful applicant was 39 year old George William Parker, Superintendent of the Belfast Fire Brigade, who was appointed in March, apparently in preference to Second Officer Baylis who was the same age and also shortlisted.

Mr. Parker made an instant impression both with the Committees and the local press. After his first serious fire, on 27th July at a former mill building on Tame Street, Ancoats, used as a workhouse and a tramp ward, Parker was praised for his efforts.

A number of people were rescued from the upper floors of the eight-storey "casual ward" by escape ladders, and six by means of jumping sheets. In one hour the building was a total wreck, but the Brigade under Mr. Parker's leadership had saved several lives under trying conditions.

George Parker had begun his career as a fireman in Salford, and was appointed Superintendent of Bootle Fire Brigade before travelling across the water to Ireland. His main claim to fame was that at both Bootle and Belfast he had replaced decrepit old premises with fine new headquarters fire stations that he had designed himself. It was no secret that over the previous eighteen months the Manchester Watch Committee had been contemplating a new chief fire station to replace Jackson's Row, and the choice of Mr. Parker, once referred to as "the architect of the world's fire service", was clearly more than coincidence. A contemporary cartoon even showed him leaving Belfast for Manchester bearing a satchel marked "plans for new station".

As things turned out, Mr. Parker arrived in the nick of time to prevent the Council building a totally unsuitable headquarters in Newton Street. The Chairman, Councillor Greenhow, was convinced that a better site could not be found, but did not reckon with Parker's greater experience. The new Chief was asked for his opinion on the proposed site and replied in a very short time with a report on its shortcomings. The report included his own plans for a seven-bay station at a new location, south of the city centre on London Road. The final plan, following closely on Parker's original drawings, was completed two years later after a design competition, and before the first brick was laid, London Road fire station was being hailed as "the finest fire station in this round world".

The new headquarters was but one of Parker's plans for the Brigade. He felt that the system of street stations was now outdated, envisaging instead a fleet of new horse-drawn escapes together with a network of street alarms wired to the central fire station.

The Watch Committee refused to be drawn on the alarm question at this stage, but in October 1899, ordered a horse-drawn escape built by William Rose and costing £145. The appliance arrived before the end of the year and was stationed at Upton Street.

New developments and changes in methods came thick and fast, and Parker's first twelve months saw some rapid progress.

One of the most important of Parker's suggested improvements arose following a turnout in October 1899. On arrival, at Mosley's Rubber Works in Ardwick, flames could be seen inside but the gates were locked. After ordering the men to break in, Parker found the works brigade tackling a fierce basement fire which ultimately required four jets to extinguish. In his report to the Committee he pleaded for legal powers to provide for breaking into premises if considered necessary. As a result, sections of the Manchester Corporation Act, passed in 1901, gave precisely these powers. The Chief Officer was to have sole charge at fires in the city, in the contributing outdistricts, and on the Ship Canal Estate, despite strong representations from Salford in whose area the major part of Manchester Docks lay.

The Ship Canal and Docks estate had been opened in 1894 but, apart from ensuring that the Manchester Brigade would actually attend in case of fire, no real fire precautions measures were laid down, despite the huge potential fire risk. In December 1899 the Canal authorities initiated talks aimed at clarifying the fire cover arrangements on

Chief Officer George W. Parker.

the estate. Chief Officer Parker's suggestions included the provision of larger water mains, a system of fire alarms, and a 4000gpm fireboat. The Canal Company provided a Gamewell fire alarm system within eighteen months but the fireboat naturally took longer and it was not until February 1903 that the Council accepted a tender of Merryweather & Sons. In the meantime agreement had been reached whereby the Canal Company paid one third of the cost and in September 1902, as a temporary measure, a Manchester fire engine was placed on board a barge at Salford Docks. The men respected Parker's leadership and this confidence was clearly demonstrated at a serious blaze at Shudehill Fish Market in August 1900. A deliberate fire in the basement, involving packing materials, subjected crews to some of the most punishing conditions they had ever known. Several firemen were overcome and had to be carried out. A total of 86 men worked in relays, repeatedly entering the acrid basement and returning with armfuls of blazing straw. All were overcome at some stage and at one period no less than twelve men lay unconscious. "Not one of the men engaged hesitated to re-enter the vault on his recovery from unconsciousness" reported Parker, and this suffering was to continue for nine hours until the fire was finally quelled.

Breathing apparatus was still sparse and it was normal for the men to suffer without protection in a "smokey job". Mr. Parker had persuaded the Watch Committee to purchase a second-hand *Vajen Badre* Smoke Helmet earlier in the year but it is not recorded whether it was used at this incident.

The Shudehill blaze, like most serious fires, occurred during the hours of darkness. In order to turn out more speedily to night-time fires, Parker introduced in October 1900, a "turnout section" at Headquarters. It was made up of an officer,

Horse-drawn escape, Upton Street, built by William Rose, 1899.

coachman and five firemen, all from district stations, together with a pair of horses already harnessed, so as to provide a much quicker response. The section, or "flying squad" as it became known, had orders to respond to all calls in the inner city area and the Ship Canal Estate.

In eighteen months, George Parker had made some significant changes in the Brigade, all for the better. His enthusiasm clearly rubbed off on the Committees, and approval was given for him to attend the Convention and Exhibition of the International Association of Fire Engineers at New York in September 1902. Such a visit by a Manchester Fire Chief was previously unheard of and it demonstrated the new thinking which Mr. Parker had inspired. The visit lasted almost two weeks and Parker returned brimful of ideas and observations. In a 30-page report published on his return, Mr. Parker noted the vastly superior conditions of the American firemen. However, what struck Mr. Parker most noticeably was the whole framework of structural fire precautions and rapid call-out systems. Street fire alarm boxes were the norm, automatic alarms, sprinkler systems and rising fire mains were installed in many of the newer buildings, and fire prevention measures in places of assembly were statutory. "We want similar laws in this country" said Parker.

Many of the ideas seen in the U.S.A. were in fact already being applied in Manchester. The provision

Upton Street Fire Station c1900 showing steamer and escape.

of an "air and light engine" to supply fresh air to special "smoke helmets" had been approved. Brass helmets (introduced only in 1897 along with wooden side-axes and sailor caps) had been changed back to leather in June 1902 because of the dangers from electricity, and much of the metalwork on appliances was being nickel-plated to minimise cleaning.

While the Chief had been in the States, the Corporation had been busy publishing a 97-page "Conditions of Service and Rules and Regulations", which had been compiled by Mr. Parker the previous year. The hardback volume was issued to every man and was the first such publication in the Department (since the separation from the Police in 1898 the Brigade had been known as "Fire Department", itself an American term).

One order still in force concerned over-the-border attendances. It was still the practice not to proceed over the City boundary (where no agreement was in force) unless life was at stake, and from time to time assistance calls from surrounding authorities put this to the test. One such incident occurred on 5th November 1902 when a serious fire caused nine deaths at Vernon Mill in Stockport. The Borough, having a Brigade of its own, had no reason to make previous attendance arrangements with Manchester. On receipt of the call, Parker ordered two steamers to proceed as far as Longsight whilst endeavouring to contact the Lord Mayor, Town Clerk or Watch Committee Chairman at the Town Hall for permission to attend. Only after finding "none of them about the building" did Parker instruct the appliances to continue to the fire.

A few weeks after the incident, the sub-committee resolved that in future, any attendance outside the city could "be left to the discretion of the Chief Officer". However, it was decided in January that the contributing authorities (Droylsden, Failsworth, Gorton, Levenshulme, Moss Side, Prestwich, Stretford and Withington) should pay the same as in-City residents for their fire service. The decision caused predictable upheaval in the townships, and the Failsworth, Prestwich and Moss Side authorities withdrew from the scheme. The others had little option but to comply. Moss Side, for whom the proposed increase would have meant a rise of nearly 400% in less than four years decided to "establish and maintain a Fire Brigade . . . independent of any other" which meant revamping completely the existing small brigade. A deadline of 24th June (when the MFB agreement lapsed) was set and in that time the Board provided a Shand Mason steamer, horse-drawn escape, horses and twelve part-time firemen under a professional chief officer, Daniel D. Sloan. The reorganised brigade operated from the Council yard until an impressive £2,000 three-bay station was completed on Moss Lane East in September 1904. Unfortunately nobody could foresee the irony of November 1904 when the brigade, including its chief officer, appliances and brand new fire station, were absorbed into Manchester through boundary extensions.

The Manchester Brigade meanwhile, had commissioned a large, new police-fire-ambulance station at Mill Street, Bradford, costing £60,000 and equipped with a horse-drawn escape. At the same time a new system of "hydraulic injectors" - a means of utilising the existing high-pressure hydraulic power main for firefighting purposes - was being installed in the city centre, and once again it was being predicted that fire engines would no longer be needed in the inner area.

Of course, fire engines - and an efficient fire brigade - would always be necessary in Manchester, despite the excellence of its water supply. The principle fire risk, uppermost in the minds of successive Chief Officers, was the central warehousing area, which was expanding continually. Indeed the progressive development along Princess and Whitworth Streets had greatly influenced Chief Officer Parker in his choice of the London Road site. The newer buildings were structurally a vast improvement on the older property but, thanks to some traditional design features and a range of very inflammable "Manchester goods" within, still took fire with alarming frequency, and the *Evening News* noted that the newer property, to the west of Market Street, seemed to have *more* fires than the older buildings around the Cannon Street area. Was there any truth, asked the paper, in the sarcasm that "a fireproof warehouse is one which gives proof that it will take fire?"

One problem was the congestion. Land was at a premium, and fire spread from one building to the next was therefore a very real danger. Captain Shaw of the London Fire Brigade apparently once said that "no fire brigade was able to cope with a fire in a building that was more than 216,000 cubic feet in extent", and yet it was said, "in Portland Street alone some warehouses are three times this size".

Relations between the Watch Committee and Chief Officer Parker became "very much strained" during 1903 after he submitted a lengthy report detailing the demoralising effect the pay and duty systems were having on the staff. Parker asked for a further twenty firemen, also a 25% pay rise for the men, whose wages had been static since 1891. The Committee ordered an inquiry into the Brigade, at the same time refusing any increase in either pay or strength. The relationship between Mr. Parker and the Committee deteriorated, and at its meeting on 3rd December 1903 the Watch Committee called upon him to resign forthwith.

The removal of Mr. Parker was followed by calls for a return to police control of the brigade. The opinions of the committee members were divided on this, but the insurance industry was "strongly hostile" to such a change. The *Evening Chronicle* was equally adamant in its disapproval of the proposal to revert and wrote: "Manchester has proved beyond dispute, not only the advisability but the absolute necessity of maintaining the position of Fire Brigade Superintendent quite independent of that of the Chief Constable." In the end, the demands to revert control were fought off and it was left to Frederic Baylis - promoted Chief Officer at the beginning of 1904 - to bring the Brigade back from the brink.

George Parker's major improvements only materialised after his departure, and 1904 saw delivery of the air and light engine and the fireboat, both supplied by Merryweather. The fireboat, appropriately named *Firefly*, was the most powerful of any British port at the time. Drawing only three feet of water, the twin-screw vessel could easily negotiate all parts of the docks.

The same year saw delivery of a turntable-ladder. This was another Manchester prototype, comprising a German Magirus ladder built on a four-wheeled chassis by John Morris of Salford, the first turntable-ladder to be made in England. The horse-drawn appliance could be extended to 82ft by means of gas cylinders. It was one of Manchester's biggest fire engines and for many years was pulled by two specially-large horses named *Duke* and *Major*.

There can be no doubt that the most fitting and lasting monument to Chief Officer Parker was the new Headquarters station on London Road, opened on

CFO F. Baylis, 1904-1916.

27th September 1906 by the Lord Mayor, Councillor T.H. Thewlis. The mighty building, which remained Manchester's central fire station for eighty years, owed much to the foresight of its planners. The triangular layout was almost identical to that envisaged by Mr Parker, but the skill of the specially-created team of architects, Messrs. Woodhouse, Willoughby and Langham, produced an outstanding design which made Manchester the envy of all other brigades. The superstructure, built by Gerrard's of Swinton, was faced in a golden buff terra-cotta in pseudo-classical style, dominated by a magnificent 130 ft. domed hose tower. On the Fairfield Street side were built seven appliance bays, all over 25 ft. wide to allow room for future occupation by motor engines. The bays were flanked by horse-stalls with electrically-operated doors. With the suspended harness, the horses could be hitched inside twenty seconds, during which time the firemen would respond from their flats on the three upper floors by means of sliding poles. To prevent any smells from the horse-boxes rising to the dwelling above, a sophisticated air-conditioning system was installed by Messrs. Musgrave of Belfast. Fresh air, drawn in from the top of the tower, was relayed to all parts, whilst foul air was extracted from the stalls, on a ten-minute cycle. Every conceivable facility was provided for the benefit of the men and their families, including a laundry, billiard room and children's play areas.

In addition to the fire station, the site included a police station, ambulance station, gas meter testing department, coroner's court and a bank. It was one of the most impressive municipal buildings in the city and, with a total cost of over £140,000, there were, not surprisingly, accusations of extravagance. The Lord Mayor, in his opening speech, defended the huge expense, saying that "whatever money had been

Moss Side Fire Station.

Merryweather horse-drawn escape, Moss Side Fire Brigade, 1903, photographed prior to delivery.

Air-and-Light appliance 1904 supplying air to smoke helmets and electric light.

spent had been well spent". An interesting link with the past was forged when, on the demolition of Jackson's Row some years later, the firemen's head keystone was taken down and installed in the tower wall at London Road.

A number of serious fires in the early 1900s showed the varying kinds of incidents - and consequent hazards - faced by the firemen. On 18th February 1906 a comparatively small fire on the Belfast steamer *S.S. Manchester* exposed crews to deadly nitric acid fumes when containers burst open. The effects were not felt until over twelve hours after the call when, one by one, the men began to collapse with respiratory difficulties.

A spectacular fire occurred on 23rd June 1908 when the relative peace of a Hulme afternoon was shattered by three explosions at the Mersey, Weaver and Ship Canal Carrying Co. Ltd. on Dawson Street. Manchester and Salford firemen, under their respective chief officers, arrived to find a 100ft long chemical store well alight, also five houses, two stables and a barge. There was considerable blast damage and a lorryload of cotton in Water Street, a quarter of a mile away, apparently burst into flames! One eye-witness reported seeing the Knott Mill railway bridge "sway backwards and forwards" and trains were halted. Despite the scale of the incident, there were only three injuries, none serious.

Unfortunately this was not the case at a disastrous lodging-house blaze in 1909 at Grosvenor Street. Many of the 250 occupants were still in bed when the fire broke out at about 8.00 am. Some were rescued by civilians and many more by firemen, by means of ladders and escapes. Two men

The fireboat *Firefly*.

jumped from the 3rd floor windows, one of whom was killed, and nine lives were lost. The inquest jury deemed it "a public scandal" that the Corporation had no powers regarding fire precautions in lodging houses.

The largest fire of this period came early on 11th October 1911 in the Davyhulme portion of Trafford Park covered by Eccles Fire Brigade, but was so close to the Ship Canal that an attendance was made by Manchester. The location was the Anglo-American Oil Company's building on Trafford Wharf Road, where 2,000 casks of lubricating oil were alight on the arrival of the three engines and fireboat. The blaze spread rapidly and soon, even the canal itself was alight, as flames spread to wooden jetties on the Salford bank. The *Firefly* "did splendid work", protecting storage tanks containing hundreds of thousands of gallons of flammable liquid, only a few feet from the flames.

Two major developments in 1911 were the commission of the "Gamewell" street fire alarm systems and the introduction of motor traction. The fire alarms had taken a long time to materialise, eleven years having elapsed since approval was given for the scheme. When the system became operational in February 1911 the twenty-circuit, 200-box network was one of the largest in the country.

The first call received via the system was to a newsagent's shop at Upper Brook Street, on 26th February, but within days of commissioning the Gamewells a problem was encountered. The public could not resist operating the alarms to see what would happen and a new social menace was born - the malicious fire call, still with us today. Before the first month had expired it was found necessary to affix to each pillar a warning notice of the penalty for misuse, namely a £25 fine or three months imprisonment.

The first motor fire engine, a 60hp Dennis appliance, was delivered in September, followed closely by a John Morris escape-carrying machine on

CFO Baylis, officers and men (and sheep!) at Jackson's Row c1905.

Supt. Alfred Tozer with a steam fire engine.

59

Belsize chassis. No time was wasted in reducing the number of horses and the first six were disposed of at the beginning of December.

The combined effect of alarms and motor fire engines meant that calls could now be dealt with much more efficiently and speedily so the number of escape huts was reduced accordingly.

It was not only the new technology that forced the closure of the street stations. Some were becoming decrepit and staff shortages brought about by the war also accelerated their demise. The calling-up of firemen into the forces (and the unauthorised volunteering of some) seriously depleted the ranks, and it was reported that Manchester's problems were amongst the worse.

Two years after the outbreak of war Chief Officer Baylis retired, to be succeeded by his Deputy, Arthur Ready Corlett. Manxman Mr. Corlett was the son of a country parson and went to sea at the age of twenty. He served as engineer with the Houston Line, working the South America runs from Liverpool, until he joined the MFB as third officer/steam engineer in 1898. His first years in office saw the brigade dealing with many problems brought about by the war ranging from financial considerations, with frequent demands for "war bonus" increases, to some spectacular and destructive fires.

The most serious fire attended by the overworked fire crews in 1916 had been in Trafford Park. On the afternoon of 29th February a fire was discovered in the engine room of the oil-carrying steamer *Spiraea*, berthed at the Anglo-American Oil Co. wharf at Mode Wheel. By the time Manchester and Eccles firemen arrived, along with the *Firefly*, a serious blaze was raging amidships. More than a

New Chief Fire Station, London Road, 1906.

dozen jets were set to work on the vessel, still laden with part of its cargo of mixed oils from Philadelphia. To avoid another disaster at the wharf, less than five years after the last one, the ship was towed down the canal to a safe mooring. Soon, however, the 316 ft oil-carrier was ablaze from end to end, becoming a total loss. The fire lasted for five days before burning itself out.

One difficulty encountered in the war was its effect on appliance deliveries. The commercial vehicle industry was heavily involved in the supply of military transport and other customers were of secondary importance. One appliance, ordered in the summer of 1917, took two and a half years to arrive, despite being locally-made.

During the war years a number of serious fires had occurred up and down the country involving armaments factories. Many of these were in sparsely-populated areas away from the protection of the big brigades. The Government was clearly worried about this for in May 1917 the City Council issued instructions at the request of the Minister of Munitions, that the Brigade was to attend fires at munitions factories *outside* the City, if needed. This may have seemed, at the time, rather a remote possibility, but, as always seems to happen, became a frightening reality only a month later. A call from the Hooley Hill chemical works at Ashton-under-Lyne on 13th June asked for assistance at a fire, concern being expressed over munitions made on the premises. In compliance with the special orders, Mr. Corlett responded with two motor pumps. In between the call, timed at 4.18 pm, and the arrival of appliances from even the Ashton Brigade, a huge explosion occurred, the effect of which was almost beyond description. The crews were met with an incredible scene of destruction. Mutilated bodies and seriously injured casualties were everywhere,

London Road Engine House, showing Chief Officer's conveyance and horse-stalls.

whilst hundreds of others were fleeing towards Ashton Moss for safety. The chemical works had all but disappeared leaving powdered bricks sticking to house walls "like snowballs". Two nearby gas holders had been destroyed along with a large cotton mill and other property. The death toll was 45 and all together 6 brigades fought the holocaust.

If a trip to Ashton seemed an unlikely excursion, then the telephone call received at 11.44 am on 2nd October must have been barely believable. The message was from Messrs. Vickers at Barrow-in-Furness reporting a serious fire at their National Shell Filling Factory at White Lund, near Morecambe and over 60 miles distant. After consultation with the Chairman of the Fire Brigade Sub-Committee Corlett ordered Second Officer Sloan to proceed with No.9 motor and eight men. On the road to Morecambe the Salford and Liverpool contingents were overtaken and one wonders what went through the minds of the crews as they passed and contemplated what they would face at the end of the two-hour journey. On reaching the scene Sloan ordered the Manchester crews to enter the premises, the first Brigade in fact to do so, and play jets on buildings and railway wagons stacked with explosives. Shells were bursting frequently and the men were instructed to take cover when the explosions occurred. Several men were knocked down by one shell burst.

The men worked in relays with the Liverpool personnel, and finally returned to Manchester on the afternoon of the 4th, fifty hours after the first call. "Owing to the initiative of the Manchester detachment", it was chronicled some time afterwards, "the great powder magazine and T.N.T. stores, and the neighbouring towns escaped being blown to pieces".

As if the death and destruction brought about through the war was not enough, a particularly tragic incident in 1917 caused even more. Fifteen bed-ridden patients died when fire swept through their hospital ward at the Delaunays Institution in Crumpsall. The ward, a single-storey wooden annexe linked to the main Crumpsall Workhouse by corridors had once been disused but was pressed into action again by wartime demand. A total of 34 women, all except one non-ambulant, were housed in the building and the surviving 19 were saved only by the heroism of the night nurses who braved the searing heat again and again to carry them outside. When Corlett arrived a few minutes later the annexe was a mass of flames and impossible to enter. The fire was spreading along the linking corridors and an immediate evacuation was ordered. That the crews managed to save the main building, already partly smoke-logged, was in itself a miracle. The fire was yet another example of the potential risk at institutional premises.

The end of the war, in November 1918, must have come as a relief to the men of the MFB. They had dealt with many large and frightening fires involving explosives, chemicals and terrible loss of life, with far fewer personnel available than in peace-time.

One of the more pleasing results of the war was the number of medals and decorations earned. At Lancaster Town Hall, in December 1918, Second Officer Sloan was presented with the King's Police and Fire Brigade Medal for his bravery in leading his men at the White Lund incident. On top of this, Messrs. Sloan and 3rd Officer Drummond both received, from the Lord Mayor, the PFBA Medal for Conspicuous Bravery- the "Fireman's V.C."- at a special ceremony in 1920. Finally, Chief Officer Corlett was awarded the OBE in recognition of his services at the many serious and dangerous incidents attended throughout the war.

Deserving though all these awards were, they contrasted sharply with the lack of ceremony shown on the occasion of a double retirement in 1919. The last two fire brigade horses, stationed at Pollard Street, were pensioned off in December as the Brigade's motorisation programme was completed and another era quietly ended.

Belsize/John Morris *Box Wagon*, photographed at London Road.

The Brigade's first motor appliance, a 1911 Dennis.

Belsize/John Morris motor pump and crew, Ash Street, c1915.

Scenes at a basement fire (address unknown) showing smoke helmet in use, and Chief Officer Corlett suffering from the effects of smoke.

Gamewell fire alarm equipment room, London Road, installed 1911.

Headquarters appliance fleet 1915, showing (*right to left*) Belsize Chief Officer's car, three Belsize pump escapes, Dennis pump, Belsize *Box Wagon* and Magirus turntable ladder.

Chapter Six

A POLICE BRIGADE

"Manchester is the most profitable city to the insurance companies in the country and they have to thank the fire brigade."

L. L. HARRIS

Fire Assessor 1928

Much of 1919 and 1920 was fraught with a prolonged pay and hours dispute which was to result in a major change in the Brigade's organisation. The end of the war, had brought hopes of, not only high pay but also an end to the oppressive "continuous" duty system, under which the men still worked an incredible 144 hour week.

The essence of the system was the "living-in" by firemen at their stations, in rent-free houses to which they resorted at meal times and after 4.00 pm, though still remaining on immediate call. There were, however, some married men for whom no brigade accommodation was available and who had to provide a house at their own expense. Their six working days, were spent at the station, sleeping at night in the sparse single quarters, and consequently away from their families for most of the week. What was desired by the men was a shift system with some completely free-time away from the station. Accordingly, in April 1919, the men submitted a claim for an eight hour day to be achieved by August. To do this the Brigade's strength of 130 men would need to be augmented by a further 230, which clearly could not be implemented overnight. As a compromise a rent allowance of 5 shillings per week for married men without Brigade housing was agreed to, also a reduction of eight hours per week and a substantial pay rise giving parity with the Police.

Although Manchester had apparently settled the matter for the time being, there was mounting discontent throughout the country with firemen's conditions and at the end of 1919 a Government inquiry, known as the Middlebrook Committee was set up to look into the problems. Among those giving evidence was Chief Officer Arthur Corlett of the MFB.

By his own admission, "one of the old school", Corlett clearly disapproved of the men's determination to enjoy more humane conditions after years of continuous duty. "Recently", he told the inquiry, "a feeling has sprung up which roughly propounds the theory that the fireman should be the hired servant of the municipality, nothing more and nothing less, his engagement is to be of a temporary nature, bounded only by so many hours work per day and so much pay".

Mr. Corlett was also against firemen joining trade unions. "Once the Fire Brigades become analogous with the ordinary branches of industry", he said, "a long farewell may be said to any continuity of action, policy of training and of general organisation . . . Esprit de Corps . . . a vital force in firefighting will vanish".

The report was published in May, the Committee's findings being that the continuous duty system was still the most efficient and that shift systems should be rejected.

The Manchester men were frustrated and angered both by the report and the Corporation's failure to make any move but were eventually prepared to accept the "two-platoon" 12-hour shift system already being operated successfully in some brigades.

The Watch Committee, anxious to reach a settlement, agreed that the two-shift system be granted to the men on condition they promise to respond, off duty, in case of any large fires. In order to accomplish this with no increase in manpower, the Fire Brigade would be reincorporated with the City Police Force.

The men agreed and swearing-in operations were completed by the following month, the new system actually commencing on December 1st. From November 18th Mr. Corlett carried the rank of Chief Superintendent, and the Second Officer, Daniel Sloan, became a Chief Inspector.

1921 found the Brigade coping with ever more dangerous and unusual fires. In April Irish terrorists set fire to five city centre buildings at gun-point after shooting a policeman, whilst in July, crews dealt with a serious blaze at the Corporation's Hydraulic Power Station on Water Street when they managed to prevent thousands of gallons of burning oil from spilling into the River Irwell. But the most significant incident of the year involved Haling's film renters at Great Ducie Street. The building was a mass of flames when firemen reached the scene, and a draper's and a hardware shop on either side of the three-storey building were also burning furiously. Three persons had already been snatched from the flames in the nick of time. Whilst the men were laying jets a violent explosion occurred in the hardware shop, and as the blaze was brought under control, it transpired that around 200,000ft of

Group of firemen at Moss Side.

Chief Officer Corlett, 1916-1931

highly flammable celluloid cinema film was stored in the premises. Miraculously nobody lost their life, but many had narrow escapes (including the firemen) and three businesses were wrecked.

Mr. Corlett immediately called for legislative powers to control film storage and to prevent the use of unsuitable premises, especially those including residential accommodation. The Celluloid and Cinematograph Film Act, passed in 1922, brought the required control over the storage and use of film.

Such pioneering and the understanding of modern fire hazards was typical of Arthur Corlett. Through the Institution of Fire Engineers, of which he was a founder member and later President, he strived to promote that technical knowledge which the profession needed to adapt itself to changing conditions. In 1924, four years after receiving the OBE, he was awarded the King's Police and Fire Brigade Medal.

The Brigade's equipment had to keep abreast of the times too and 1924 saw the delivery of an impressive new turntable-ladder and four new smoke helmets. The latter were given a severe test at a difficult and punishing fire the following January, when the Brigade, along with Salford, was called to the 3,000 ton freighter *Chinese Prince*, about to discharge her cargo of Egyptian cotton at No. 9 dock. A serious fire was developing in Number 2 hold and despite the application of thousands of gallons of water from the *Firefly* the cotton continued to give off dense and acrid fumes. Firemen, wearing smoke helmets, forced their way into the hold but the helmets only gave limited protection, and for upwards of four hours the crews suffered harshly.

Ford fire tender and crew, Pollard Street c1920.

Leyland Metz turntable ladder, 1924.

"Despite the choking fumes and intense heat, firemen went down to the seat of the outbreak", said one reporter, but ". . . with the heat of the helmet and the furnace-like atmosphere it was a physical impossibility to stay there more than a few minutes at a time". Throughout the incident Chief Superintendent Corlett, and Superintendent Ashbrook of Salford continually descended into the hell-hole to direct operations. Afterwards Corlett pleaded for and got more smoke helmets.

The *Chinese Prince* incident was the first serious ship fire to be attended by the *Firefly* under a new arrangement. When the vessel was commissioned in 1904, a third of her cost was found by the Manchester Ship Canal Company, whilst the Corporation paid the rest, and this arrangement continued with regard to the maintenance costs. In November 1924 control of the *Firefly* passed entirely to the Company, the seven crewmen, consisting of three Captains, two Engineers and two Auxiliary Firemen, being transferred with her.

The *Firefly* had been one of the Brigade's best investments, and since 1904 had seen action at over 40 serious fires involving ships and dockside property. She was to last another eleven years, until the Company replaced her with a new tug/fireboat, also called *Firefly*, in 1935. It was said that in all her 31 years, at least one boiler had always remained ready for instant turnout.

A new fire station being erected at Great Jackson Street, was to be the first to be built solely for motor appliances, and the increased use of motor cars generally was causing the Committee concern. Mr. Corlett's opinion was that motor garages were a "serious risk", and that the not inconsiderable quantity of petrol contained in vehicle tanks, and not covered by legislation, added to that risk. The problem was remedied somewhat by new regulations in 1928.

Fires involving any flammable liquids are always potentially disastrous and present special problems for firemen. The brigade at this time had little in the way of suitable extinguishing media, only foam extinguishers. These had been used to good effect in August, at a serious incident at the Bradford Road Gasworks, where an alarming and violent explosion had wrecked two gas-holders and caused many injuries. The Brigade had to deal with burning tar and gas pockets around the remains of the gas-holders, at great personal risk to crews. But larger petrol and oil fires could not be adequately dealt with by means of hand extinguishers and firemen invariably had to struggle against the odds with water jets.

A fierce fire in 1925 at the Southern Cotton Oil Company Ltd. in Trafford Park, involving barrels of oil and grease, raged for seven hours before finally burning itself out. The following year, an explosion at an oil works in Plymouth Grove, started a disastrous fire which spread to an adjoining factory and a house. Several oil drums exploded and eye-witnesses reported seeing injured and screaming women workers fleeing into the street. The body of one unfortunate woman was found on the top floor by firemen who had been held back by "intense heat". It was no doubt with these experiences in mind - and the attention drawn to garage and petroleum fires - that the Brigade purchased its first continuous foam generator in July 1928.

The Brigade continued to develop its equipment to cope with changing fire conditions.

After a serious ship fire in December 1929, at which teams of firemen in smoke helmets worked for four hours to no avail it was decided to phase out the helmets and replace them with modern breathing apparatus. Shortly after this incident the first Siebe Gorman "Proto" sets were purchased. With their own self-contained supply of fresh cool oxygen the new sets allowed firemen to move unhindered around a smoke-filled building.

It was a reflection on the pace at which fire technology was changing that it had been less than five years since the *Chinese Prince* fire at the same dock, after which Mr. Corlett had pleaded for more

Great Jackson Street Fire Station during World War II.

smoke helmets, yet now their total replacement was being planned.

Early in 1931 a brand new vehicle, constructed in the Brigade workshop on a 30 cwt. Chevrolet chassis, was commissioned to carry the new sets, the remaining smoke helmets and other special equipment. Described as a " fast travelling rescue van", it was the forerunner of what is now known as the "emergency tender".

Mr. Corlett retired at the end of March 1931 with over thirty-two years service. His last serious fire, on 21st March, involved a six-storey building in Mosley Street, in the City centre. The one hundred year old block, of typical Manchester "lightwell" construction was used by several firms as offices and warehouses with a basement cafe, where the fire started. The mid-day blaze, one of the largest in Manchester for many years, soon drew a huge crowd as seventy foot flames leapt from the roof.

At the height of the blaze, Mr. Corlett was on the roof directing operations when "in a moment of excitement", his false teeth fell out and landed on the pavement below. Not to be outdone, he shouted to a policeman on the street who, to the amusement of the onlookers, retrieved the offending dentures and took them back up to their owner. On recovering his teeth, the Chief Superintendent washed them in water from a branchpipe, replaced them, and carried on with the job in hand. "That was a narrow escape" he said afterwards. Despite his smoke-eating reputation, Mr. Corlett was remembered more as a pioneering fire engineer who greatly advanced the science of firefighting.

There was never any doubt as to who was to succeed Mr. Corlett, and on 1st April 1931, Second

MP15 Dennis/John Morris pump escape, London Road, 1929.

Officer Sloan took charge of the Brigade.

Daniel Devine Sloan, a Liverpudlian by birth, had begun his fire service career at Bootle in 1893, but his first firefighting experience occurred even before then. At the age of about fourteen, whilst serving as an apprentice seaman, on a voyage from New York to Shanghai, his ship became crippled in a storm and had to drop anchor. Whilst thus marooned, and with the nearest land, the West Indies, five miles away, young Sloan spotted smoke coming from the hold. Although knowing that the old windjammer was carrying a highly flammable cargo of oil, he volunteered, together with the ship's carpenter, to enter the smoke-filled compartment, extinguish the flames and so save the vessel and her crew. One can only wonder at what would prompt so young a person to take such a brave course of action, but this fearlessness was to remain with him throughout his service.

He was once quoted as saying that a fireman's greatest fear was that of catching pneumonia at fires, something which happened to him no less than three times. There was certainly nothing else on the fireground which ever frightened him and he was several times referred to as "the man who can't be killed".

In 1903 he became Chief of the Moss Side Fire Brigade and was transferred into Manchester the following year. His succession to the post of Chief Superintendent on 1st April 1931 was marked by a real "baptism of fire" as the Brigade had one of its most hectic periods for a long time. After taking over officially at midnight, the rest of the night and much of the following day was taken up with a number of serious outbreaks around the City. There could not have been a more fitting start to Mr. Sloan's career as Chief Officer.

As if the Brigade did not have enough to do, a determined gang of arsonists at large in the late twenties and early thirties made sure that there was plenty of extra work for the Manchester firemen. The fire-raisers, led by Mr. Leopold Harris, a dishonest fire insurance assessor, were responsible for a whole string of serious factory and warehouse fires in Manchester, London, Leeds and other places. All the fires were started with the intention of making fraudulent insurance claims, most of which were duly over-assessed by Mr. Harris, who secured a sizeable reward on each occassion. Many of the businesses involved were specially set up with the intention of being destroyed by fire, and were usually insured for a figure far higher than their true worth, often with the aid of false records and dummy goods.

The first fire to be started by Harris's team, in November 1927, involved a silk importers - Fabrique de Soieries Ltd - on Deansgate, the proprieter of which, Mr. C.V.L. Capsoni, was one of the original gang. Fortunately for the fire-raisers, the MFB

Chief Superintendent D. D. Sloan seen wearing the many decorations earned during his illustrious career.

returned the cause as "light dropped" which conveniently allayed suspicion. Several other serious fires, of which the largest in Manchester was a five-storey warehouse in York Street, occurred before the gang was finally crushed by painstaking detective work. At the Harris trial, no less than tweny-nine fires were mentioned as having been started deliberately and apart from the later ones, when the net was closing, the cause had originally been thought accidental in most cases. Of course, the art of fire investigation was nowhere near as advanced as it is today, nor did forensic science play such a prominent part in criminal investigations. In addition, the skill of the arsonists, and the fact that fires in clothing warehouses in cities like Manchester were frequent occurrences anyway, gave the Harris gang a long run of successes before being finally tracked down.

The thirties saw a rapid rise in housing developments in Manchester, notably the spread southwards in the new Wythenshawe "satellite" estate beginning to take shape. Unfortunately, the nearest Manchester fire station was at Moss Side, several miles from the new estates, and a plan was prepared for a temporary police and fire station on Altrincham Road, Sharston, with twelve new homes being reserved for firemen. The station became operational in May 1934, with a Station Officer and ten firemen being transported daily by lorry until their accommodation was ready.

1934 proved to be a busy year for the Brigade; a total of 1119 responses were made, just short of 1933's 1122 record figure, and of that total, a record 966 actual fires were extinguished. Once again, the largest incidents were in the City centre and Trafford Park.

The *S.S. City of Adelaide*, berthed at No. 8 Dock and about to unload the largest cargo of Indian cotton ever received, was involved in a severe fire in April. £10,000 worth of cotton was lost before brigades from Manchester and Salford were able to quell the blaze.

1935 brought another record turnout figure, coupled with a rise in fire losses. The most costly fire was undoubtedly the blaze at the C & A department store on Oldham Street, in January. The blaze which began in the kitchen raged for three hours before being controlled and caused £40,000 damage.

Mr. Sloan tendered his resignation in November 1935, to take effect early the following year. He had been in the Brigade for thirty-one years, since the takeover of the Moss Side Fire Brigade. Accepting his resignation, the Watch Committee noted that "the whole of his distinguished career had been marked by undaunted courage and unfailing devotion to duty". Mr. Sloan was one of Britain's most illustrious fire officers and the epitome of every young boy's hero. He was the man who led

Handing over of a new Merryweather turntable ladder appliance — Albert Square 1934.

Manchester firemen into the Morecambe munitions horror of 1917, and who had snatched more people from flames than could be recorded here. His list of decorations awarded over a forty-two year career could hardly be surpassed: Kings Police Medal, the medal of the Professional Fire Brigades Association, three Royal Society For The Protection of Life From Fire silver awards, the Watch Committee Medal for Bravery and several commendations. In 1933 he became the first officer to be both Senior Vice-President of the Institution of Fire Engineers and the President of the Professional Fire Brigades Association at the same time. In short he was the most heroic and celebrated fireman ever known in Manchester, and his comparatively short term as Chief Officer, due of course to Mr. Corlett's longevity, hardly did him justice.

Mr. Sloan's Deputy, David Drummond, the Scotsman originally appointed as Fourth-Officer Motor Engineer in 1917, replaced him as Chief Officer on 1st April 1936 at a salary of £650, rising to £850 per annum.

Soon afterwards the Chief Constable took the opportunity to restructure the Senior Officers along police lines. Mr. Drummond would be designated Chief Officer and the other senior officers would become Superintendents, Inspectors and Sergeants. This would clearly recognise the fact that firemen were members of the police force.

One problem with the old system had been that at night there was no higher rank on duty than Station Officer, which meant alerting the Chief Officer and Second Officer for every call. Now, any one of three inspectors would be available, and so responsibilities were delegated more sensibly.

The establishment of the Brigade in 1936 was one-hundred-and-sixty, all ranks, but with the two-platoon system, only around fifty men could be mustered at a time, when rota days and sickness were accounted for. At a recent fire, in Trafford Park, every on- and off-duty member was in attendance, coping with an extraordinary fire

£40,000 fire at the C&A store, Oldham Street, January 1935.

situation during which they continued to relieve each other for twenty-four hours. A request for an extra twelve men in 1937 and a further twelve in 1938 was acceded to.

No doubt the exceptional circumstances of the Trafford Park incident had a bearing on the decision to increase the Brigade's strength. Probably the largest of Trafford Park's many serious blazes, this latest one had broken out on 8th July 1936, just as thousands of workers were leaving the Park on a hot sunny evening. A passing tram-conductor, spotting a small flame in one corner of a large timber shed on Trafford Park Road, stopped the car to raise the alarm. Before he had returned to his tram that flame had engulfed the complete shed and was spreading, literally like wild fire, fanned by a stiff summer breeze. Three simultaneous calls were received at Headquarters just after 5.00 pm and an ominous pillar of smoke was visible soon after turning out. The first response comprised two motor pumps from Headquarters and one each from Moss Side and Great Jackson Street stations, with the Chief Officer in charge. On arrival, two huge timber yards, a large warehouse and several other buildings were already well alight. Practically the whole of a seven acre sight between Trafford Park Road and Westinghouse Road was ablaze from end to end and the firemen's task seemed hopeless at the outset. Reinforcements were immediately sent from all over Manchester and Stretford and the fireboat "Firefly" was called out to relay water to the motor appliances. The intense heat given off by the blazing timber stacks made attack at close quarters almost an impossibility. The firemen sheltered behind stacks of timber not yet involved and played their hoses through the gaps between them; others built barricades of empty oil drums. One fire appliance had to be continually sprayed with water whilst pumping and an ambulance speeding through the fireground, with an injured civilian, was still warm when it arrived at Salford Royal Hospital. The Trafford Park Estate Office was saved only by virtue of its steel window shutters which were kept cool with spray jets. The following morning, the full scope of the devastation was clear. Water from thirty-nine firefighting jets had completely flooded the area, so that the sleeper roads were turned into huge floating wooden rafts. The total damage to property included the two large timber sheds of Messrs. Rosser and Messrs. Watson & Todd, massive outside timber stocks, the storage warehouse of Messrs. Jabez Bennett and the Southern Oil Company's empty drum store. A train of thirty-three wagons had been reduced to a tangle of twisted metal, and little remained untouched over the seven acre site. Telephone and tram wires had been brought down and a dozen marooned tramcars stood idle. Five civilians and three firemen were treated at hospital and many others had their uniforms scorched. Altogether, over 30,000 tons of timber had been destroyed and the damage totalled £350,000.

The fire had been the first major incident attended by Mr. Drummond as Chief Officer. What he could not have known was that he would be the last Chief Officer of the Manchester Fire Brigade in its existing form, and that however extensive that particular fire had been, it was nothing to what he and his men would be facing in the next few years.

1934 Merryweather turntable ladder at London Road Fire Station, photographed shortly before the Second World War.

Chapter Seven

THE BLITZ

"Fatigued almost beyond endurance by their efforts, sodden and frozen by the cascades of water ... they worked on."

OUR BLITZ: RED SKY OVER MANCHESTER

Kemsley Newspapers Ltd, 1944

The month of July 1936 saw the publication of a report by the Riverdale Committee which had been appointed by the Government in 1935 to inquire into the organisation of fire services in England and Wales. Among its recommendations were the consolidation of fire service legislation and a statutory requirement on all local authorities to provide a free fire service. With one eye on the deteriorating international situation at this time the Committee called for area mobilising schemes and the building up of reserves of equipment to cope with possible air raids.

The Manchester authorities already had such matters under consideration. Its emergency fire scheme, completed at the end of 1937, proposed a force of 300 auxiliary firemen, 46 emergency fire stations and £18,000 worth of extra equipment including twenty motor pumps and ten trailer pumps. The Government's Air Raids Precautions Act of 1937, took effect at the beginning of 1938 and laid down the financial arrangement for auxiliary fire services nationally.

In Manchester a number of distinguished laymen were appointed as executive officers of the Auxiliary Fire Service (AFS), and training commenced in April. In July the Council's new Air Raid Precautions Special Committee met for the first time. The firefighting services of Manchester would now be in the hands of two committees, the Watch Committee which administered the regular brigade and the ARP Special Committee which dealt with the AFS.

In July 1938 a new Fire Brigade's Act came into effect which laid down a number of specified fire authorities, giving them two years to either provide a fire service or else make suitable arrangements. This did not of course affect places like Manchester, although the local authorities of Stretford and Urmston, protected by the City brigade, did take steps to form their own joint fire service as a result. The main effect on Manchester was a requirement that charges for firefighting services would cease within two years. Thus ended the long and sometimes stormy relationship between the City Council and the combined insurance offices.

The emergency firefighting plans were progressing favourably. Under a new AFS plan approved at the end of 1938, there would be 55 emergency fire stations and a revised auxiliary establishment of 6,662. Of these over 1,600 men had been recruited already.

Although the auxiliaries were still lacking in

fireground experience, the regulars had been given a rare taste of things to come when three bombs exploded in the city centre around dawn on 16th January 1939. Unfortunately the Brigade, along with the Police, the public and officials of the corporation gas and electricity departments in whose underground services the explosions occurred, were not immediately aware that the blasts were of nefarious origin, short circuits in the mains cables being blamed. However, police investigations led to the arrest, two days later, of a number of Irishmen in connection with the incident. Over the next twelve months the spasmodic activities of Irish terrorists in various cities, including Manchester, were to bring unwelcome problems for the emergency services just at the time when they were preparing for a somewhat more organised conflict.

An opportunity for the auxiliaries and regular firemen to work side be side came when a disastrous fire ravaged part of the prestigious Kendal Milne department store in February 1939. During the firefighting operations many members of the AFS reported to the scene to volunteer their services and the Chief Constable expressed his satisfaction with the blending of regular and auxiliary personnel.

The emergency fire pumps were still arriving and causing problems of garage space. The now-disused Pollard Street fire station was being utilised to house some of the new equipment but the very lack of space that had brought about its closure in 1938 meant that it would be of limited use, and in the early part of 1939 pumps were standing in all weathers in fire station yards. Eventually, storage space was found at the former LMS Carriage Works in Newton Heath.

The AFS also needed an administrative and training centre and the ARP Special Committee agreed to a £35,000 conversion of the former St. Joseph's Industrial School at Stockport Road, Longsight. This had a spacious yard area and a four-storey administrative block and so was ideal for AFS purposes.

As the international situation continued to worsen Sir Harry Haig was appointed the North Western Regional Commissioner, and a Regional Fire Inspector was to be installed at Arkwright House in Manchester to co-ordinate fire appliance movements in case of war.

In late August Chief Constable Maxwell announced that plans for the police force, the wardens and the fire brigades were ready to be put into immediate operation if necessary. On 1st September, Germany attacked Warsaw and AFS personnel were summoned to duty as an indefinite "blackout" was imposed across the country. Under new Regional Orders Fire Brigades were grouped into districts, within regional areas; in the North Western (No. 10) Region Manchester became the centre of No. 4 District, also comprising the brigades of Salford, Eccles, Irlam, Sale, Stalybridge, Hyde and the embryo Stretford and Urmston Joint Fire Brigade. The idea was to give the Chief Officer of (usually) the largest brigade in

Chief Officer Drummond, 1936-1941.

Ten pumps and four special appliances fought this blaze at the prestigious Kendal Milne department store, Deansgate, in February 1939.

the district, in this case CFO Drummond, the power in times of emergency to mobilise appliances from any of the stations in that district to the area where they were most needed.

As expected, forty-eight hours after the ultimatum was given to Germany to withdraw from Poland, Britain found itself at war and the Manchester AFS was mobilised "with speed and efficiency"; all fifty-five stations - some of them barely completed - were occupied and the new training-school at St. Joseph's commenced operations. About half of the authorised AFS strength of over 6000 had already been enrolled and recruits continued to arrive. Despite this flurry of activity the expected attack did not come at that time, nor even that year, and there was a feeling of anti-climax.

Over the border, the new Stretford and Urmston Joint Fire Brigade commenced operations on 1st November and Manchester finally stopped providing fire cover in those districts, including the giant Trafford Park industrial estate, that had been the scene of some of MFB's biggest fires. One month later the Brigade stopped attending the Ship Canal estate also, so that for the first time in many years the MFB was only responsible for calls within its own boundaries.

The months of "phoney war" brought about a drop in both the morale and strength in the AFS. This was principally due to the calling-up of men into the armed forces, though a number of whole-time auxiliaries had resigned due to the wages and - if the truth was known - boredom.

The acquisition of suitable cars and lorries for towing duties was also causing problems due to a shortage of vehicles and arrangements were made to hire second-line towing units at a suggested rate of 4/0 to 4/6 per hour.

News concerning the AFS firefloats was more promising and on July 22nd the *AFS Mancenian* hastily "took the water" - minus the usual ceremonies - and proceeded to Potato Wharf to join her sisters the *AFS Mancunian* and *AFS Lancastrian* for duty on the Irwell and the city's canals.

Exactly a week later the first bombs fell on Greater Manchester, landing in the Ordsall district of Salford. This first attack, though causing only minor damage, nevertheless heralded the beginning of the air-raids - at the end of August the action began in earnest. On the night of the 28th bombs struck an oil-storage site near Altrincham, Cheshire, and the mutual assistance scheme had its first test when the resultant serious fire necessitated movements of appliances and foam from Manchester into the adjacent No. 3 District. The following night Hulme and Moss Side were hit and it was to be the residential areas of Manchester and the surrounding towns of Salford and Stretford which bore the brunt of the raids which gradually increased in severity towards the end of the year as the Luftwaffe attempted to destroy the Trafford Park Industrial Estate, the Docks and the great manufacturing complexes around the City.

As the raids continued throughout September Chief Officer Drummond pinpointed an area of serious deficiency in the City's defences. Drawing attention to the dangers of incendiary bombs hitting unoccupied city-centre buildings, he urged a twenty-four hour patrol of all commercial and industrial premises. The Fire Watchers Order 1940 issued the same month, made such patrols obligatory, but only in certain classes of premises, and was thus of limited success.

AFS crew under training.

Mr. Drummond's words were to be of particular significance as later events were to prove.

Throughout the rest of 1940 the bombing continued on a regular basis and Manchester's firemen saw much action. The auxiliaries had to do a twelve-hour stint of duty one night a week and report into their stations on the sounding of an air-raid warning. However, due to the frequency of the raids, this latter requirement soon proved to be too exhausting, and an odd/even date system of alternate nights was adopted instead. Nevertheless, many AFS men still responded to air-raid warnings on their off-duty nights.

During this period several other cities had been the object of full-scale *Blitzkrieg*, attacks when the Germans launched major raids destroying large areas of the town centres and inflicting severe casualties.

Mobile columns of fire appliances from Manchester were involved in several regional moves, travelling to Stoke-on-Trent, Liverpool and the West Midlands. It seemed only a matter of time before Manchester's turn would come, and there was an atmosphere of inevitability in the City. On 20th December Liverpool was hit and Manchester appliances were moved across under the regional mobilising scheme.

While the contingents were still in Liverpool, the enemy suddenly switched its attack to Manchester. On Sunday 22nd December the sirens sounded at 6.37 pm, but this time it was different. The events of that night and the following one would be etched into the memories of Mancunians for many years to come.

Three minutes after the warning the first fire call was recorded as incendiary bombs rained down in their thousands. From that time calls were received "with increasing speed" and within ninety minutes every available fire appliance - including redundant hand escapes - was committed. A request for assistance was quickly passed to the Regional Fire Inspector at Arkwright House, but he was already "harassed" due to there being three separate heavy attacks in the No.4 District (at Manchester, Stretford and Salford). However, reinforcements were soon organised and at one fire, on Deansgate, the first appliance there was from Marple, Cheshire. The thirty pumps and 200 men which had been despatched to Liverpool were hastily called back, but in the days before radio telephones this was no mean feat. Some of them, already fatigued from their exertions in Liverpool, were redirected to Stretford before actually reaching Manchester. Further reinforcements were ordered from other regions and hundreds of firemen began to converge on Manchester. Before the night was over more than 170 appliances from as far as Cardiff, Birmingham and Newcastle would be in attendance.

As the attack continued and the incendiaries did their work of piloting the bombers which were to follow with high explosives, the number of fires rose alarmingly. Soon the sky over Manchester was one huge red glow, which could be seen for miles, as one after another the large city-centre buildings - many of them devoid of fire watchers - burst into flames. Regular fire officers were detailed to make their way from one incident to the next, pausing only for a few hurried instructions - and no doubt some words of encouragement - before leaving the scene in the hands of ordinary firemen as they sped to the next outbreak. The task seemed virtually impossible; sometimes on turning a corner an officer would find a whole block of warehouses, on two sides of a street, in flames and only a handful of auxiliary trailer pumps available with which to fight. Only the toss of a coin could decide where to begin and at one such situation in Miller Street the choice was made to start on one particular side; whilst the crews began working on the chosen warehouse the buildings on the other side of the street were suddenly shattered by a bomb!

Water supplies, never usually a problem in Manchester, were heavily taxed due to the number of pumps at work and the destruction of water mains. In addition, communications were disrupted due to enemy action and great reliance was placed on motor-cycle messengers. All the time bombs

Painting by Ron Henderson of the 1933 Leyland Pump Escape.

Dennis/John Morris & Sons pump, 1935.

Leyland/Merryweather Turntable Ladder, 1940.

Scenes from the Christmas Blitz 1940. *above*: The corner of Portland Street/Parker Street (Barlow & Jones' Warehouse). *below*: the view across Piccadilly. The buildings in the foreground are surface air-raid shelters.

Ex-NFS Austin Heavy Unit rebuilt in the Brigade Workshops as a salvage tender.

Heyscroft NFS No 10 Regional HQ.

Ex-NFS Foam Tender after complete rebuild in Brigade Workshops (see also photograph on page 95)

London road Yard c1950.

Mobile Deluge Set.

continued to fall, placing crews in mortal danger. "Throughout the night the Fire Service stood up to their task", said the official report, "with the result that the continued efforts showed signs of success towards morning".

When the "all-clear" finally sounded some twelve hours later the situation was improving; by 11.30 the next morning the fires were reported to be under control. Due to the vast scale of firefighting operations there were no fresh men available to retrieve the crews, and so the men who had been at work all night had to remain on the streets "damping down" for the rest of the day.

Unfortunately the enemy returned that evening with a second devastating attack. Pumps were still scattered all over the City centre, the hose was wet and the crews were completely fatigued; nevertheless they rose to the occasion, attacking the fresh incidents with "vigour and spirit". The second night's raid was every bit as heavy as the first. Once again incendiaries were dropped which soon illuminated the City and provided the necessary target for the following bombers, although with many fires still showing a light from the previous night's raid, their task was made very much easier. The appliances and men already out on the streets were quickly mustered, their equipment made up and brought into London Road for re-direction as required. As supporting appliances arrived from outside the City they were rendezvoused at the AFS Headquarters at Longsight and sent to London Road in batches of ten; some pumps were even drafted in from London.

The raid proved to be shorter than the previous night's but in some ways was more severe. Parachute mines were dropped onto the City and, according to reports, Nazi planes tried to machine-gun some of the firemen. The "all-clear" was heard

A building on George Street, Piccadilly, burns furiously during the Christmas Blitz, 1940.

at around 1.30 in the morning; an hour or so later every fire was reported to be surrounded and it seemed that the Brigade had again mastered the flames.

However, Manchester had other enemies besides the Germans that night, for at 3.00 am a strong north-east wind suddenly arose and whipped up the smouldering warehouses and other buildings into raging infernos once more, the flying brands setting alight some large blocks which had suffered nothing more than broken windows in the bombing. Within half an hour huge fires once again raged across the City centre.

The heart of the conflagration was a huge area of warehouses in the congested commercial area surrounded by Piccadilly, Portland Street, Mosley Street and Oxford Street and pumps were quickly concentrated here. In the centre of this vast site stood two buildings which were of vital importance to the City: these were the main telephone exchange in York Street and the electricity works in Dickinson Street. Fortunately, pre-planning had taken these two risks into account and a system of "fire stops" had been previously drawn up. Even then the fierceness of the blaze drove the firefighters back to the "reserve stand" in Abingdon Street and a hasty on-the-spot decision to demolish one warehouse in Charlotte Street by means of explosives was taken. The fire was arrested at the eleventh hour and the two buildings saved; by 2.00 pm on that Tuesday - Christmas Eve _ the Manchester Blitz was finally controlled.

The cost had been enormous. Over two nights, nearly 600 lives had been lost in the Greater Manchester area, including 64 members of the emergency services and Civil Defence. The bomb damage had been devastating; more than 800 high explosive bombs and 32 parachute mines had been

Aftermath of the Blitz. The scene in Parker Street on the morning of 24th December 1940.

above: Fireman John Leonard escaped with minor injuries when falling debris destroyed the Metz turntable ladder after a 'direct hit' during firefighting operations, St. Mary's Gate.
at right: Though the raiders have gone the firefighters are still at work. Christmas Blitz, 1940.

counted as 270 enemy aircraft reached their target. In the City centre, over 30 acres had been affected and some of Manchester's finest buildings lay in ruins. There was widespread damage in the residential districts too; it was calculated that altogether 50,000 properties had been damaged in Manchester alone.

Fire service casualties had been severe: George Albert, a regular fireman, lost his life in Piccadilly along with several AFS colleagues as high-explosives fell near to where they were working, and over 100 men, both regular and auxiliary, were injured, some seriously.

Fifty pumps and two turntable-ladders were put out of action; two AFS temporary stations were destroyed completely and lesser damage caused to other stations.

A total of six "conflagrations", twenty major fires and 600 lesser incidents were recorded by the MFB Control over the two nights. At the same time Salford suffered heavily, and there was severe bombing in Stretford and other nearby towns.

The fire service had performed magnificently, despite the AFS being some two-thirds *short* of its authorised establishment. Not surprisingly a number of Manchester firefighters later received decorations. Auxiliary Fireman Arthur Stoakes who rode his messenger motor-cycle for 104 hours through the thick of the Blitz with petrol cans strapped to his back and who was twice blown off his machine received the BEM, along with Chief Inspector William Smith who continued to direct operations after being injured; and so too did Auxiliary Fireman Mawdesley who piloted two firefloats through the bombing, fighting waterside fires beneath walls which were threatening to collapse. Sergeant William France and Temporary Sergeant Andrew Whyte also received the BEM and Fireman W.E. Burgess had a commendation published in the London Gazette.

But as well as bringing deserving awards to the firemen, the Blitz taught Mancunians some serious lessons. Despite the Fire Watchers Order of 1940, many buildings had been without protection in their hour of need, either through exemption or mere default. The Manchester authorities joined those of other cities in demanding action.

Another problem encountered in the Blitz was the

AFS personnel and self-propelled pump at Crumpsall Hospital AFS station.

reliance placed on mains water supplies in urban areas such as Manchester. Bombing and the loss of pressure due to over-drawing had highlighted the fact that even Manchester's water mains had their limitations. To provide further static supplies, the basements of a number of blitzed buildings were cleared out and filled with water; some of these such as the Parker Street warehouses site, could hold over half a million gallons.

The Brigade learnt many valuable lessons during the two nights of the Blitz and the improvements and alterations made afterwards were to stand it in good stead in later raids.

It had also been found during the Blitz that, due to an insufficiency of officers, auxiliaries were left on their own at some incidents. To prevent this situation recurring the regular officers were dispersed amongst the AFS stations, and regular sub-stations. Under the old system all the senior officers had been resident at Headquarters, so that a pump-escape appliance from London Road responded to every incident in the City for the sake of officer-cover and its wheeled escape. This was inconsistent with the divisional set-up introduced with the AFS. Spreading the Inspectors and escape-carrying appliances around the Brigade made for a much more efficient method of operation.

There was growing dissatisfaction in the AFS at this time over conditions at the City's temporary stations. At one, the domestic facilities comprised one small room with no beds, no cooking facilities, no toilet, no water and no heating, and which was shared by twenty men. There were also reports of stations being infested with bugs.

Further controversy came with "a bold attempt" in December 1940 to place the fire brigade on a separate footing from the police. Describing CFO Drummond as a "most excellent officer", Alderman Hall said that he was "no more than a cypher" under the present system and could not be deemed a "fire chief" in the way of London and other cities. The Chief Constable (Mr. Maxwell) could not be expected to carry out both functions efficiently it was said. But the motion was defeated and within a few months the issue would become irrelevant.

The enemy action did not stop with the dawn of a new year, and the Manchester fire services continued to attend incidents in the early months of 1941. In May, two AFS men were killed when a bomb exploded outside their temporary station at Birchfields Road Bus Depot. The 1941 raids had not yet been on the scale of the Christmas Blitz, but a sharp attack on Whit Sunday tested the Brigade's revised procedures to the full.

Wartime MFB uniform, including steel helmet and respirator.

It was in the early hours of June 2nd that a heavy raid was launched on the Manchester area, the worst since December. Thankfully, only one night of *Blitz* action took place, but the casualties and destruction were on a large scale. Once again the incendiaries were dropped in large numbers and serious fires soon raged, chiefly in the City centre and just to the north of it in the congested areas of Strangeways and Cheetham. The bombs which followed brought much devastation with direct hits on the Jewish Hospital and Salford Royal Hospital, causing severe casualties, The Assize Courts at Strangeways were completely destroyed by fire and many other public buildings, including the Police Headquarters in South Street, were hit in varying degrees.

135 separate fires were recorded in the City but the experience of the Christmas raids had helped considerably. Despite the fracture of the 30-inch Godley water main at Ashton Old Road, supplies were maintained and the water storage basements were put to good use. Regional movements of appliances were quickly organised and soon nearly seventy appliances from as far afield as Liverpool and Runcorn were arriving to render assistance to the Manchester men, thirty of whom were injured during firefighting operations.

Although the Fire Brigade had once more risen to the occasion, it would be untrue to say that severe strains had not been inflicted on the fire services in cities like Manchester during the raids.

There was increasing opinion that fire defences should be organised on a national footing, as a kind of fourth arm. In the months between the Christmas and Whitweek raids on Manchester moves were afoot to unify all the fire brigades in the country into one co-ordinated force. On 18th August 1941 the National Fire Service (NFS) was formed and the MFB ceased to exist albeit temporarily.

The formation of the NFS promised unified control of firefighting resources, greater mobility of appliances with standard sized units of command, together with standardisation of training, equipment and administration.

A national Civil Defence network already existed and the NFS was organised within the same regional boundaries, a Chief Regional Fire Officer taking charge of all the firefighting resources in one particular area. The Headquarters of the North Western Regional Civil Defence Commissioner were already in Manchester, at Arkwright House, Parsonage, and so it was natural for the North Western (No.10) Region of the NFS to have its base at the same address. Lt. Cmmdr. John Hampden Fordham RN (Ret'd) was appointed CRFO for the region.

The No.10 Region was divided into four Fire Force Areas (Nos. 26-29) of which No.27 Fire Force comprised the cities of Manchester and Salford, the large county boroughs of Stockport, Oldham and Rochdale, and over 50 other former fire authorities from Buxton in Derbyshire to Whitworth in Lancashire. Almost straight away it was realised that this area was far too large and within a few months the Derbyshire portion was transferred to another Fire Force, the first of several such boundary changes to which No.27 Fire Force was subjected over its relatively short life.

A large detached premises known as Moseley Hall, situated in Cheadle, a suitably safe distance from the City centre to escape air raids, was selected as Fire Force Headquarters, wherein Mr. Francis Dann, the Fire Force Commander took up his duties.

Chief Officer Drummond, with over 24 years service in the MFB behind him and within sight of his retirement, was offered nothing more than a senior administrative post. Such a position clearly did not appeal to a city fire chief with the operational record of David Drummond and he declined accordingly. His termination date was postponed until February 1942 for pension purposes but Mr. Drummond never actually took up any duties in the ensuing months. It was an inappropriate and somewhat sad end to the career of a man who had risen through the ranks from Motor Engineer to Chief Officer and had piloted the Brigade through its most trying period with dedication, skill and honour.

Many changes were made to Manchester's firefighting organisation under the NFS. Operationally the number of temporary fire stations was increased and some of the worst ones replaced. Other premises were opened such as Divisional Controls and Sub-Controls, and several new fireboat stations were commissioned. In addition many buildings were requisitioned for various administrative purposes such as transport and pay, associated with the City's position as both a Regional and a Fire Force centre.

A continuing programme of vehicle replacement was undertaken, and new appliances - albeit of utility design - began to appear to replace commandeered or pre-nationalisation equipment worn out by over twelve months of enemy air-raids.

The NFS was formed to cope with large-scale firefighting situations brought about by enemy action. In fact, after the summer of 1941, there was a marked reduction in the bombing over Britain and the NFS, particularly in the north, was never really tested in the circumstances for which it had been designed. There was further bombing in Greater Manchester, some of it severe, but the worst of the raids was over. The most noteworthy incidents then in the lifespan of the Manchester NFS concerned non-enemy action fires. Of these, one tragic incident stood out as being the worst Manchester fire, in terms of casualties, for over 100 years.

In the small hours of Wednesday 11th February 1942, as nearly 100 guests were asleep in the city centre Deansgate Hotel, a small fire started in the basement. The outbreak went undetected at first due to a lack of fire patrols but at about 5.00 am one guest was aroused by the smell of smoke and reported it to a young night porter. Unfortunately, the 41 staff on duty that fateful night had not been trained in any fire routine, and nobody thought to call the fire service or alert the firewatchers in the basement garage. By now the fire was spreading and involved several ground floor rooms. The acting manageress, Miss Stevenson, woke up and was able to knock on the doors of several residents before having to make her own escape.

As the smoke steadily filled the corridors and crept into bedrooms, more guests were roused and soon scores of people were fleeing the building in blind panic. Some found the corridors lead to dead ends and had to retrace their steps, other found their way out thwarted by locked doors, but some did find their way through onto the roof. The fire hoses were grabbed to try and fight the developing fire, but in some cases they were not even connected, and to add to the confusion the lights failed making escape that much more difficult. It was not until 5.27 am that somebody thought to call the fire brigade.

About the same time, Police Sergeant Herbert Dainty, on patrol in Bridge Street, several hundred yards down Deansgate, suddenly saw flames in the direction of the Cathedral. Sprinting along the street he arrived at the six-storey building to find the front of the hotel well alight, with numerous residents perched on window sills crying for help.

Just then the NFS arrived and immediately raised a turntable ladder to pluck the terrified victims from the windows. Sgt. Dainty and PC Ernest Stott then ran round to the rear of the hotel where an extension had been built backing onto the River Irwell. On entering the extension the two officers found 30 people trapped by a locked door at the foot of the fire escape and released them by smashing the glass. As firemen rescued some 29 people from the upper floors at the front by turntable, supporting appliances began to converge on the doomed hotel until 20 pumps and 124 firemen were on the scene; two fireboats were turned out and arrived alongside the rear walls. Meanwhile the two police officers attempted to force an entry on the fourth floor, but

The Deansgate Hotel. *left*: River frontage showing knotted bedsheets still in position.
right: Deansgate frontage where turntable ladder rescues were carried out.

were driven back by the flames and intense heat. Eventually they managed to enter the floor below and, against the odds, dragged out seven survivors from the raging inferno.

As the fireboat crews trained their powerful searchlights onto the rear windows, knotted bedsheets appeared at the third floor, followed by two men, one elderly, climbing down. But the end of the improvised rope was 40ft above the murky waters of the Irwell and the firemen shouted a warning. Both men slipped, one being immediately swept away by the current; the second was dragged from the water by the fireboat crew. Another victim climbed down his knotted bedclothes but could only reach the third floor, where he clung to a window-sill until firemen fought their way through the flames to rescue him.

Three firemen were injured and a young firewoman fell 30ft through the garage roof. The fire tore through the building causing the floors and the roof to collapse. The following morning only a smoking shell remained.

On the Thursday firemen began a top-to-bottom search of the ruins and the police dragged the river. A senior police officer said, "We may never know how many people, fearing their escape to the ground floor was cut off, leapt from the windows at the rear of the building into the swift flowing River Irwell, in the darkness, before the arrival of the fireboats". The search went on for days, the Civil Defence Rescue Parties finally completing the task. To complicate matters, the junior night porter to whom the fire had first been reported fled the City and a moorland search was initiated. Identification and accounting for the victims was going to be difficult; the hotel register had been destroyed and several bodies were burned beyond recognition. It was finally established that 16 people had lost their lives on that disastrous night, but only 14 bodies were recovered; five of the victims were located at the bottom of a shaft down which they had stumbled in the darkness.

Before the casualties had even been counted there were demands in the House of Commons for an inquiry and the Home Secretary, Herbert Morrison, called for a full report. The cause of the fire was the subject of much speculation. Nearly 20 years afterwards theories were still being propounded that a "fifth column saboteur" had deliberately started the fire with an incendiary bomb to cover up either the murder, or kidnapping, of one of the guests, a government official, whose body was never found. However, this theory was discounted by a number of experts who had been involved at the time.

At the inquest, held three weeks after the fire, there was severe criticism of the abysmal fire precautions in the hotel and a verdict of misadventure due to civil negligence was recorded. Nobody would ever forget the tragedy and as if to make sure the charred skeleton of the building was to stand for nearly 30 years in one of Manchester's main thoroughfares, a stark reminder of the importance of fire precautions in residential buildings.

Aside from such drama, there was much routine work for the NFS to do and progress to be made. The Service had to be prepared for the enemy to return at any time with raids of the kind that had brought about the nationalisation. Accordingly firemen were kept busy maintaining static water dams, drilling and taking part in exercises.

Much of the frustration at the lack of enemy action was compensated for by a war productivity scheme in which firemen and women were engaged in a wide range of essential tasks to aid the war effort. A staggering quantity of weaponry, radios and countless other items were either assembled, polished, inspected or otherwise processed, and when this scheme ended in 1945, it was calculated that over 300,000 man hours had been devoted by 27 Fire Force personnel on vital war production work.

27 Fire Force underwent its second major change in September 1942 when all the remaining Eastern

side was reformed into a new Fire Force, No.42, with its Headquarters at Stalybridge. The same month saw the Regional Headquarters move from Arkwright House in the City centre to *Heyscroft*, a large house in suburban West Didsbury.

In an organisation the size of the NFS movements of staff were not uncommon and the following year Chief Regional Fire Officer Fordham was transferred to the Home Office, his place at No.10 Region being taken by Lt. Cmmdr. K.N. Hoare RN (Ret'd) who was also ex-London Fire Brigade.

A Dartmouth graduate, Cmmdr. Hoare had served as a sub-lieutenant on submarines until an accident caused him to retire prematurely from the Navy in 1937. Looking for another career he had joined the London Fire Brigade as an Assistant Divisional Officer, and when the Blitz came he took charge of operations north of the Thames.

Towards the end of 1943 large-scale movements of NFS personnel took place as firemen and firewomen were drafted to the south of England to strengthen defences in connection with plans for the invasion of Europe. From about this time the strength of the NFS in the provinces was to be gradually decreased as the war moved in a different direction and the threat of attack or invasion became less. Blackout regulations were eased in September 1944 and firewatching duties were relaxed at the beginning of 1945.

The official end to hostilities provided for even greater reductions in the Service, including the closing of many temporary firestations. It was not yet possible to revert completely to prewar manning levels as firemen were still required for the dismantling of emergency water tanks and similar work.

A further reorganisation of 27 Fire Force in the summer of 1945 put all remaining 11 Manchester stations into one division with a view to a smoother denationalisation. One station, Pollard Street, Ancoats, which had enjoyed an unexpected second lease of life during the war, having originally been

Winners of the Women's Regional Pump Drill Competition held at St. Joseph's, April 1942.

Visit by HRH King George VI to Regional HQ, Heyscroft, November 1942.

NFS 27 Area HQ ladies day held at Moseley Hall c1943.

closed in 1938, finally closed its doors in 1946.

A new Fire Services Act of 1947 provided for the desired denationalisation which took effect from 1st April 1948, but only the larger county boroughs and cities, including Manchester, would be permitted to become fire authorities: all the remaining areas would have fire brigades administered by the relevant County Council.

One of Manchester's first tasks was to find a new Chief Officer. The Council selected Cmmdr. Hoare at a starting salary of £1,350 per annum. Kenneth Newcome Hoare proved to be an excellent choice as Chief Officer and turned out to be one of Manchester's greatest fire chief "characters"; his professionalism, enthusiasm, dedication and delightfully individual personality, made him one of the most well-liked and respected chief officers in the country.

Within weeks of his appointment being announced in October 1947, the Chief Fire Officer designate reported on the proposed establishment of the new Brigade. It provided for a total of nine stations (the two remaining temporary stations at Sherborne Street, Strangeways, and John Street, Gorton, being no longer required). A strength of 331 full-time personnel was envisaged with a front-line fleet of thirteen pumps, one emergency tender, two pump-salvage tenders and three turntable ladders all constantly manned. Other equipment to be manned on a second-line basis included a foam tender, canteen van, control unit, hose-layer and breakdown lorry.

In January 1948 the other senior officers were appointed. Joseph Whiteside MBE, a prewar Manchester fireman and Assistant Fire Force Commander in the NFS turned down the post of Chief Officer at Kingston-upon-Hull to become Deputy Chief of the Manchester Brigade. Windsor P. Jorgenson was appointed Third Officer with the rank of Divisional Officer Grade I, the other Divisional Officers being Eric Ashworth and Albert Dunleavy. Arthur Smithson, who had worked his way up through the NFS administrative sections after being seriously injured as a fireman in the Blitz, was appointed Chief Clerk. All these officers were, in fact, former Manchester firemen. The senior management team commenced the task of re-establishing the MFB with enthusiasm and no doubt some trepidation.

On 31st March 1948, one hundred and fifty men and six appliances paraded through the City centre, with the salute being taken by the Lord Mayor, Ald. Miss Kingsmill-Jones, on the Town Hall steps. Although pre-empting the official change over date by several hours, the NFS was stood down from that moment in everbody's mind and the MFB was born again.

CFO Kenneth Newcome Hoare, 1948-1968.

NFS Stand-down parade, Albert Square, 31st March 1948. The salute was taken by the Lord Mayor, Alderman Miss Kingsmill-Jones.

Chapter Eight

REBIRTH

"It is not sufficient to maintain an efficiently manned and equipped Brigade unless it is used towards a reduction of fire loss by prevention of fire."

CFO HOARE
Annual Report 1950.

The Brigade was organised into three divisions, of unequal size. Central Division, under the command of Third Officer Jorgenson, comprised the central high-risk area and included only the Headquarters station at London Road. The rest of the City was divided into North and South Divisions, centred on Mill Street and Moss Side stations respectively.

The operational personnel worked a two-shift, sixty hour week system, which had been in vogue since 1947. Average pay for a fireman, after two years service, was just over £5 per week.

To comply with the obligations of the Fire Services Act a Fire Prevention Department was established, under Assistant Divisional Officer Edward Hibbitt. In those early days the Department's work was largely confined to education and publicity, goodwill inspections - (which had no legal "teeth") - and dealing with requests for advice.

The control and communications centre of the Brigade was based, naturally, at London Road and by the end of 1948 the new MFB had dealt with 1295 calls. The principal method of receiving these calls was the exchange telephone, which accounted for about half of the total; the two other main methods were the police telephone and the street fire alarm.

The 231 Gamewell boxes had been installed almost forty years previously, but were still considered by the Chief Officer to be the best system in so far as they transmitted details of the call to all stations simultaneously and did not rely upon a spoken message. The authorities, swayed by Cmmdr. Hoare's conviction that the street alarm was worth keeping at all costs, agreed to his suggestion of a campaign to promote the system and hopefully reduce at the same time the number of malicious calls. The campaign was launched in January 1949 and received much publicity, resulting in a temporary increase in awareness, and the usual helpful suggestions from the public, such as automatic handcuffs to detain a caller. Signs continually updated by operational crews, were affixed to certain boxes stating the number of times they had been improperly used, and the reward for information leading to an arrest was increased from £1 to £5. At the same time the boxes were repainted from their original red to yellow and black, so as to increase visibility.

The Committee agreed to extend the alarm system and at the same time convert the Gamewell Room at Headquarters into an up-to-date Control centre, with speech-recording equipment for the 999 calls.

opposite: 2-way radio, 1948.

In the early years after denationalisation, a great deal of effort was put into developing both the public relations and the social and competitive side of the Brigade. A station efficiency competition was instituted together with a technical quiz, pump contest and the "Tweedale Shield" first aid competition. For the public there were "At Home" weeks, exhibitions and a major event at Platt Fields in 1950 comprising displays of every type of appliance. Unfortunately, though publicly a huge success, the show was marred by an industrial dispute caused by the event itself. However this was overshadowed the following year by a national "spit-and-polish" ban, remembered in Manchester for the Chief's decision to replace suspended men by officers, recruits, civilians and firewomen.

The development and character of the Brigade through the 1950s reflected the personality of Cmmdr. Hoare just as much as the late nineteenth century period showed the influence of Alfred Tozer. This manifested itself in many ways, the street fire alarm campaign being typical. By 1952 the programme of updating the system was well advanced. Thanks to the determination of Cmmdr. Hoare and his useful connections with the London Fire Brigade, the Corporation had purchased over 250 alarm heads from the capital. The London heads - withdrawn due to persistent misuse - were amongst the most modern in the country and Manchester's "scoop" scored a point for Cmmdr. Hoare in the for-and-against-alarms controversy which raged at this time through the pages of the technical press. In July 1952 the complete system was closed down for two months so thast the new heads could be installed and several pillars resited.

1951 saw the Commander touring several

A street fire alarm in operation.

Brigades in Belgium and Denmark. Whilst abroad, he was particularly impressed by some features of the Continental appliances and on his return made strenuous efforts to design and build a similar appliance in Manchester. The four appliances already commissioned since 1948 proved to be the last "standard" models ever purchased by the MFB for, with just a few exceptions, all those delivered afterwards were to the Brigade's - or perhaps more accurately, Cmmdr. Hoare's - specifications.

The first of the "Manchester pattern" fire appliances was a pump-escape of unique design planned for delivery in the financial year 1953/4. As a result of the Chief's ideas, special permission had been obtained to import, via Dennis Bros., a two-stage high/low-pressure pump, manufactured by Carl Metz of Germany. The new appliance was to have a Dennis chassis with Rolls-Royce petrol engine (as normal) but fitted with the German pump - front mounted - and bespoke bodywork. Numerous technical problems had to be overcome, including the designing of a special new chassis by Dennis, but by the autumn of 1953 the vehicle was ready for bodybuilding. It was at this point that Rolls-Royce, taking advantage of the forward-mounted pump which obviated the normal power take-off, offered to fit - on a trial basis - an experimental American-made gearbox with two-pedal control. The device, built under licence, had previously been fitted to Rolls-Royce cars but this would be the first such gearbox in any commercial vehicle. Approval was readily given and, after construction of the bodywork by a small coachbuilder (the start of another Manchester tradition) the machine went "on the run" in 1954.

The summer of 1953 saw two major incidents being attended by the brigade, each of a completely different nature. In the first, the crews responding to an early-morning call on the street fire alarm system had no idea what was to greet them at Smedley Road, Collyhurst, just outside the city centre. The sight on arrival beggared description: two trains had collided almost head-on, high on a viaduct over the River Irk. The 7.36 steam train leaving Victoria Station for Bacup had run into an electric train just arriving from Bury. Such was the force of the impact that the Bury train had plunged off the bridge into the River below, where one coach came to a halt standing on end. A huge rescue operation was mounted and altogether some ten persons lost their lives with sixty injured.

The second call came less than a week later, and involved a large mineral water factory of Jewsbury and Brown, at Ardwick Green - the most serious blaze attended by the Brigade since reorganisation.

A novel development at this time was the Brigade band, which was formed in 1953 utilising the profits from a successful technical quiz book called "Focus on Fire". In the following years the band became a familiar sight at civic events in the City, but due to a decline in both players and finances, was forced to disband in the 1970s, despite a marriage-of-convenience to the Central Manchester Band from Clayton. The quiz book remained successful, however, and was translated into several languages.

The overseas element was a notable feature of the post-war MFB particularly as the training school increased in stature. In 1954 two officers from Bombay attended the school and set the pattern for an association and reputation with foreign Brigades which was renowned. The broad-mindedness and enthusiasm of the much-travelled Cmmdr. Hoare resulted in officers from all over the world coming to Manchester to receive instruction. To reciprocate the training of overseas personnel as it were, many Manchester officers spent periods of secondment in places such as the Persian Gulf, and West Africa, teaching British expertise and methods, or assisting in the setting up of new fire brigades.

London Road Fire Station where the School was based, was by now nearly sixty years old and the Committee decided that such a milestone in the history of one of the Corporation's finest buildings should not go by without celebrations. The Committee were, with some justification,

Post-war Austin emergency tender, formerly a World War II rescue appliance.

Ex-NFS Fordson foam tender prior to rebuilding.

MFB Silver Band, resplendent in white helmets, at Moss Side.

exceedingly proud of their fire brigade headquarters. It had lived up to all the superlatives written about it in 1906 and was easily able to accommodate the latest motor fire appliances in its roomy engine house.

The Golden Jubilee Celebrations took place on Saturday 6th October 1956, the culmination of a week-long programme of activity in the form of Open Days and other events.

The pristine condition of the Headquarters building had been carefully maintained by means of an annual exterior spring-clean which was part of MFB tradition. Every May for many years, the week-long washing-down of the terra cotta had been carried out by the firemen using ladders, trestles, hose and a soft soap mixture known as "soogee". However, following representations from the Union, the final wash-down was carried out in 1957.

That year, the City's rapidly-developing airport at Ringway was the scene of a major disaster. Just after lunch on 14th March 1957, the BEA Viscount *RMA Discovery* was arriving fron Schipol Airport, Amsterdam, and making the usual approach from the north east towards Runway 24. Just as it was about to cross Shadow Moss Road something went terribly wrong, and "Discovery" suddenly swerved violently, turned turtle and ploughed into a row of houses, immediately bursting into flames. Two houses were completely demolished, and a third engulfed in flames. Airport fire crews, seeing the aircraft in difficulty, were reputedly mobile even before the impact and within three minutes, seven crash tenders were on the scene, including two from the Fairey Aviation Company's Brigade at Ringway. Appliances from Cheshire and Manchester Fire Brigades were close behind and Cmmdr. Hoare himself took charge of the firefighting and rescue operations. All twenty passengers and crew on the Viscount had been killed and two persons were trapped in the houses which had collapsed on top of the wreckage. The *Wythenshawe Recorder* in its Editorial said the disaster "must go down as the

The Irk Valley train smash, 15th August 1953.

Withington Fire Station and appliances.

The Brigade's first post-war delivery, a Dennis F7 received in 1950.

The 1954 Dennis F18 fitted with Metz high/low pressure pump and Bankfield coachwork seen at Great Jackson Street.

Dale Street fire, 1960.

Manchester Fire Brigade stand at the fire exhibition, Olympia, London, 1965.

A Dennis F24 appliance.

Moss Side Fire Station.

Handing over of a new Hydraulic Platform appliance, Moss Side, 1972.

Moss Side's new Hydraulic Platform appliance is put through its paces, 1972.

tragedy which struck at the one place where it had for a long time been expected".

The major fire hazards in Manchester were still the large number of old warehouses, shops and industrial property in the congested central areas. The Fire Prevention Department, as it was now known, continued to make its laborious progress, persuading the occupiers of premises to improve their fire precautions, still without the backing of proper legislation.

Unfortunately, the measures taken were often insufficient to save a building, particularly if the construction and contents were conducive to a rapid fire spread. One such building was the Paulden's department store on Cavendish Street. An automatic alarm system had been installed, on the Brigade's advice, and it was this which brought three appliances racing to the building on the evening of Sunday, 8th September, 1957. The Station Officer in charge found a rapidly developing fire on the first floor. Assistance was quickly requested, but the fire continued to roar through the 90 year-old building, unhindered by compartmentation or sprinklers. Twenty minutes after the first call the store was burning from top to bottom. Cmmdr. Hoare arrived soon afterwards to find the blaze still spreading. Not liking the look of the two lofty frontages along Cavendish Street and Cambridge Street, he ordered all his crews to withdraw to the corners of the building. This decision probably saved the lives of several men, for soon afterwards both these walls came spectacularly crashing down. However, the Brigade Chaplain was on hand to say "a special prayer for the courage and safety of the fire

Pauldens fire, 8th September 1957.

squads", and so perhaps the credit was not all due to Cmmdr. Hoare! The famous Paulden's clock-tower was next to crumble and by 8 pm the store was a smoking ruin, with water from three turntable ladders, two ground monitors and fifteen hand jets still playing. Afterwards, Cmmdr. Hoare warned that the City was full of similar blocks, and urged the protection of buildings by compartmentation, fire-resisting construction and automatic fire alarms, none of which were compulsory at this time.

The Paulden's fire delayed the attendance of the Cmmdr. at the annual conference of the Institution of Fire Engineers, due to open the following morning in Southport, at which he was to be invested as President.

The conference was the start of a glorious year for Kenneth Hoare, in which he achieved much for the IFE, the Manchester Fire Brigade and his own reputation, culminating in a richly deserved award of the Queen's Fire Service Medal in the 1958 Birthday Honours list. The "highlight" of Cmmdr. Hoare's presidential year, to use his own words, was a visit to the Conference of the International Association of Fire Chiefs in Los Angeles, at which he delivered an address.

The largest and most spectacular fire of Cmmdr. Hoare's memorable year occurred in January 1958, and was noted for a remarkable feat of firefighting under the Chief Officer's command. The Brigade was turned out by a nightwatchman to a fire in a ballroom and restaurant at Belle Vue Gardens. The block, which was nearly 600 ft. long, was built entirely of wood with an asphalt roof, and it was certain that any fire which gained a hold here would be virtually unstoppable.

When the first appliances entered the gardens, the fire was already burning fiercely and being whipped up by a strong wind. So phenomenal was the rate of spread that a miniature "fire-storm" was being created and there seemed little chance of saving the building. A turntable ladder was quickly deployed to the 80 ft. high water-chute, where flying brands had ignited the woodwork.

The adjacent King's Hall was being used for the Belle Vue Circus, and the animal trainers hastily led horses and other animals away as a precaution. But

Water curtain in position to protect the lion house (*left*), Belle Vue, January 1958.

The prototype Leyland/Carmichael Firemaster seen *(right)* on test at London Road and *(above)* dealing with a fire in the Strangeways area, 4th April 1969.

the worst threat, at the leeward end of the inferno, was to the lion house which stood directly in the path of the roaring flames. In that building, apart from the lions, were the leopards and a rare and valuable tigon. As the windows cracked and the paint blistered zoo officials braved the searing heat to enter the lion house with rifles ready to shoot the cats before the fire reached them.

While the leopards paced nervously around and the lions lay bewildered in the corners of their cages the battle outside was intensifying. Cmmdr. Hoare, realising the inevitable outcome if the fire jumped the 20 ft. roadway, suddenly took the decision to reposition his jets into the space between the two blocks. The result was a solid "wall of water" which prevented the flames from reaching the lion house.

But as the firemen struggled to maintain the barrier, a single shot was heard inside the lion house: the strain and panic had proved too much for one of Belle Vue's oldest inhabitants - Judy, a 17-year-old lioness - and it was regrettably decided to put her down. It was a particularly sad decision to make as Hoare's water curtain was successful and the lion house was saved. All that remained of the 4,000 seat Coronation Ballroom, the Tudor Suite and the Baronial Hall was a pile of charred timber.

1958 saw two major developments in Manchester, both of which were strongly influenced by the unceasing enthusiasm of Kenneth Hoare. The first was the advent of a completely new type of fire appliance which would always be associated with Manchester.

In looking for the right manufacturer for the next generation of pumping appliances a unique liaison was struck with Leyland Motors Ltd. At the invitation of Cmmdr. Hoare, the firm joined forces with the Brigade to produce, from the drawing board stage, a brand new chassis, embodying all the features which had been pioneered in Manchester such as a front-mounted major pump, high-pressure hose reels and automatic transmission, but utilising a diesel engine. The new model was given the name *Firemaster* and was unlike any previous fire appliance. The 150 bhp engine was underfloor-mounted, centrally between the axles, leaving the front clear for the pump; and a semi-automatic transmission, featuring "fingertip" gear changing, was fitted. Over the next few years three pump-escapes and one emergency tender based on the Leyland were commissioned, all four giving excellent service for many years and serving their purpose in the way that only own-design equipment can.

The other major event in 1958 was the passing of a local act which included some important new fire prevention measures. Cmmdr. Hoare was particularly concerned about certain risks for which no adequate legislation existed already. These included the many buildings of excessive height or cubical extent without any structural fire precautions, other premises with inadequate access for fire appliances, and the increasing use of oil-burning equipment and neon signs. Having an eye also on the exciting high-rise developments planned for Manchester, he urged that all new buildings should be compulsorily fitted with built-in protection such as sprinklers. The fires at Paulden's and the Deansgate Hotel had highlighted the problems of poor compartmentation and access; whilst oil-fired boilers, many of which were crammed into basements and other inaccessible places without adequate separation, had been responsible for a number of serious fires in Manchester. Nevertheless, there were strong objections from the oil and construction industries to the proposals, resulting in the Chief Officer being called to give evidence before a select committee. But the authority won the day and the Act received Royal Assent in December. It was probably the first local enactment to combine so many far-reaching powers, but, being principally aimed at the modern buildings could not be generally applied to the many old, high-risk properties which had been responsible both for its introduction and for most of the large fires to which the Brigade was called.

One area of the city containing a high proportion of such buildings was Ancoats, once the city's last great cotton-spinning district, but now a declining twilight zone of slum housing and run-down industrial

Fog shrouds the Flatley's mill fire, 10th February 1959.

premises, many in multi-occupancy. This area was the scene of a huge blaze on 10th February, 1959, which occurred on one of the most memorable evenings of the Brigade's history. Manchester was enveloped in thick fog when fire broke out in the former mill in Pickford Street, occupied by several firms, notable Flatley's Ltd. The building, known as Long Mill, was a typical Ancoats factory: a vast, ugly, seven-storey block surrounded by narrow thoroughfares. The fire started, on the first floor, and four employees of a handbag factory, working late, were cut off by smoke. Although the fog slowed the Brigade's arrival time, and disguised the signs of fire, the four trapped workers were quickly rescued by ladder.

Divisional Officer Harry Lomas, in charge of the first attendance, soon realised that the fire was assuming serious proportions and, without further ado, ordered the number of pumps to be increased.

Back in the Control Room calls for assistance were quickly passed to the surrounding brigades and further appliances were drafted in to Manchester stations in case of additional calls. Supporting crews converging on the City found themselves hampered by the fog and attendance times were severely affected. After one hour, the situation at Flatley's was "critical". Three turntable ladders and fourteen jets were already in use with virtually the whole building now involved. As the fire raged out of control, the little terraced houses clustered around the mill were hastily evacuated; and radiated heat and sparks started fires in adjoining property. The situation in the Control Room was equally critical with so many appliances on the road but, as the night wore on, the mobilising situation became almost impossible. Three minor calls before midnight - including one malicious false alarm from a street box, on, appropriately, Fog Lane - received less than the customary attendance in view of the situation.

The "stop" message, denoting that the situation at Flatley's was in hand and that no further help would be needed, was sent at 11.29 pm, but thirty minutes later, and with twenty-five pumps, five special appliances and two AFS pumps still on the fire ground at Ancoats, the street fire alarm panel burst into life. Box No. 64, at Oldham Street in the City Centre, and only 400 yards from Flatley's Mill had been actuated for another serious fire at Lyon's Cafe in Stevenson Square. On hearing of this new development Hoare, who was still directing operations at Flatley's, immediately redirected some appliances from there to assist at Stevenson Square where the fire was rapidly spreading to Burton's the Tailors. The fear that an arsonist was at large, taking advantage of the dense fog, was compounded minutes later when several repeat calls heralded another fire at Marsden Square, just a few blocks away. The Stevenson Square fire, with the accompanying request for ten pumps, meant that Control had to scour further and wider for appliances and further calls exacerbated the situation.

In all some fourteen appliances from outside Manchester were called to the Flatley's fire alone, apart from the standby pumps and those attending Stevenson Square.

The few short years up to 1960 saw a number of major fires, but one incident stood out as probably the largest and most famous fire in the post-war

The end of an era. In 1959 Cmmdr. Hoare recommended that Manchester's 253 street alarms be taken out of service due not only to the increased number of GPO telephone boxes but also to the large number of malicious alarms (898 in 1958).

years of the Brigade.

The Dale Street fire of 18th October 1960 occurred in a huge warehouse in the Rochdale Canal basin, in the heart of the City centre. The building, erected in 1822, was owned by the Canal Company, though sub-let to several firms who used it for storing furniture, rubber, cotton and other materials.

The interior was a classic example of a building "built to burn". Open staircases and hoistways connected all floors and provided a ready passage for the spread of fire. It was the kind of place which had brought about the fire provisions of the 1958 local Act and if the legislators needed to show any further proof of why those powers had been sought, then this building would give it. Access for fire appliances comprised only the short frontage on Dale Street and the one side which looked onto the yard.

By the time the fire brigade had been summoned soon after 10.00 pm, the furniture warehouse on the first floor was alight. Appliances were driven into the yard but lorries and cars completely blocked the access. With flames now belching from most of the windows and the fire appliances beginning to scorch, the offending vehicles were already warm as firemen and volunteers pushed them clear. Beneath the lorry park was a 1500 gallon underground petrol tank and the front door was blocked by a blazing fuel oil tank. As paint drums exploded around the firemen a house immediately adjacent to the building was hurriedly evacuated.

The building was alight in no time on all floors and the firemen, under the command of the Chief Officer, were sent clambering over rooftops to check for fire spread. Assistance was brought in from as far as Oldham and Stockport, until thirty appliances were eventually on the scene. Locating the incident would not be difficult for the supporting crews - the City Centre was bathed in a red glow reminiscent of the Blitz and which could be seen from ten miles away. At the height of the blaze, three men were injured when a section of wall collapsed. After three hours, the fire was declared under control, though still burning fiercely. Water from twenty-five medium jets, three radial branches, four turntables and two ground monitors continued to pour unceasingly onto the blazing pyre. At one stage lock gates had to be opened to let more water in as firemen pumped a section of the Rochdale Canal dry.

In the morning light the 140 year-old warehouse was a smoking ruin, and the few remaining walls were ordered to be demolished. The debris continued to smoulder for weeks afterwards. The cost of the fire, which had been deliberately started, was £758,000 and it had been the most serious peace-time fire in the city in living memory. Cmmdr. Hoare, commenting on all the operational problems it had caused, summed it up when he said, "Without a doubt, this is the most difficult and worst fire since the Blitz".

The Dale Street fire, 18th October 1960.

Chapter Nine

THE FINAL YEARS

"The quality of service traditionally rendered by firemen in Manchester springs from its history."

Chief Fire Officer Harry Lomas

Annual Report 1973

The Dale Street fire highlighted yet again the problems caused for the Brigade by the numerous old warehouses and industrial buildings which abounded in the City. Despite Manchester's progressive local legislation the fire prevention staff admitted they were almost powerless to deal with the situation.

The Fire Prevention Department was going through something of a transitional phase. From its early post-war days, specialising in publicity and goodwill advice, the Department was now taking on more of an enforcement role as responsibility for various inspections passed from the City Architects Department to the Fire Brigade. It was also a period of rapid advancement nationally in the fire prevention field with fire disasters at Keighley, Bolton and Liverpool leading to successive enactments.

A tragic incident in Manchester in 1962 demonstrated graphically how helpless the Brigade was without sufficient information to act upon, and how necessary it was to work closely with other services.

Shortly after 1am on 19th September a fire call was answered in the Control Room, but before the caller could pass on the address he suddenly broke off. Repeated requests for the address were unanswered and the GPO operator, still monitoring the call, was immediately requested to have it traced. All that could be heard on the other end of the line were terrifying shouts and screams indicating that people were trapped in the blaze. Eventually, after an agonising 130 seconds, the operator reported that the call had been traced to a newsagent's shop in Hulme and immediately pumps were turned out from Great Jackson Street, Moss Side and London Road.

The blaze was a serious one, resulting in the loss of three lives, and clearly the two-minute delay while the address was being checked had been critical. At the Coroner's inquest, three months after the incident, the fire brigade tape recording of the initial call was played, an unusual and unprecedented step allowing the fire victims to present their own evidence, as it were.

The tape recorder had been installed in 1953 and, although never having been used in such a dramatic way before, had proved itself very helpful to the Control staff by giving a useful second chance to hear an unintelligible call and assisting in the prosecution of malicious callers. The MFB was well known for its innovative measures in the field of mobilising and communications, due in no small way to the resourcefulness of the Brigade's communications officer, Harvey Scattergood.

For three years, Mr Scattergood had been working on a new remote control call-out system for the district stations, which was probably the first of its kind in the country. This would obviate the need to relay fire calls by telephone and would relieve the station dutyman of the task of handling fire calls. (It was normal at this time for one man per shift to be designated as a non-riding dutyman, looking after the watchroom. When the man whose turn it was could not be spared from his riding commitment (e.g. the only driver on duty), then a non-qualified junior would drop off the appliance and relieve the dutyman when required. This man was always referred to by the Manchesterism "Pudicof" because his job was to "Pick Up Duty In Case Of Fire").

The technical problems which had to be overcome were considerable. The station bells and turnout lights were operated from Brigade Control at London Road and the location of the fire passed by a public address system using post office lines. Facilities had to be provided for "running calls" (where a person arrives at the station to report a fire) and for those calls received by automatic fire alarms linked to the sub-stations. Both of these methods of raising the alarm required a fully-manned watchroom (in case the appliance was already out). The former problem was solved by providing a telephone outside each station, linked directly to Control. The latter problem was ingeniously dealt with in typical MFB fashion. When the street fire alarm system had been discontinued in 1959, a number of mechanisms were retained and subsequently used as relay devices to transmit AFA calls from their original termination points in the sub-stations to the Control Room at Headquarters. Each AFA line was allotted an old street alarm circuit. This could then be relayed along the wires, in its number code, to a receiving apparatus at Headquarters from where it could be

Brigade Control, 1962, showing, in the background, the tape-recording apparatus.

dealt with. As automatic alarms came into greater use in the following years, their termination points were transferred to commercial alarm centres away from the fire stations. Unmanned watchrooms are the norm today, but in the early sixties, the MFB system, was well ahead of its time.

One of the largest fires of the period occurred on 8th March 1963, in the City centre warehouse district in Major Street which, despite its name is a narrow backstreet, flanked on either side by tall buildings. The six-storey warehouse was in the centre of a row of similar properties occupied by various firms, the majority of which were associated with the textile trade. Access was therefore severely restricted and could be gained only from the front and rear of the premises so that the positioning of jets and turntable ladders proved to be extremely difficult. Showers of sparks and burning embers were whipped up into the air by strong winds and, if allowed to go unchecked, could have started a chain of fires in a number of nearby buildings.

Throughout the night over 120 firemen from five brigades, with twenty pumps and three turntable ladders, fought the inferno against almost impossible odds, but successfully saved the surrounding property.

A new system of call-out for major fire situations enabled a reduction in the working week from 56 hours to 48. In approving the 48-hour week to start from April 1963, the Brigade obtained the Union's agreement to operate an emergency call-out system in case of large fires. Up to five pumps could be fully-manned in less than ten minutes by sounding a special bell signal at London Road to alert the resident men, and by calling others on specially installed telephones in their homes.

Unfortunately in the early part of 1963 the Brigade did not have five spare pumps available. A sharp increase in fires had taken its toll of the fleet, and, as the reserve appliances ran out, second-hand appliances were purchased from the neighbouring Lancashire Brigade.

Despite the adoption of the new duty system the

Leyland Firemaster emergency tender and equipment, 1962.

The Major Street fire, 8th March 1963. Flying brands whirl high above the surrounding property.

establishment had remained the same, thanks to the new measures such as the remote control turnout and other efficient arrangements but recruiting was still far from satisfactory. By the end of the year the actual brigade strength was still some 43 men short. The introduction of a "Junior Fireman" cadet scheme in 1963 helped matters by "bridging the gap" between school-leavers and the minimum recruiting age of 18.

An incident towards the end of 1963 spotlighted attention on yet another aspect of the Brigade's training role, namely the Auxiliary Fire Service. Since recruiting began in late 1949, the Manchester AFS had been steadily built up to nearly 200 men and women. A training centre functioned at Moss Side fire station where, three evenings a week, the volunteers attended for instruction. On most nights riding crews were organised to man the green Home Office appliances attached to the Brigade and these crews were allowed to attend fires in order to consolidate their training.

One of these riding crews, responding to a fire call in Wythenshawe, was involved in a serious accident just after turning out from Moss Side in November 1963. The AFS appliance, collided with a fully-laden double-decker bus in Princess Road, killing two of the auxiliaries outright and throwing the rest of the crew into the roadway. More than thirty people on the bus were injured to some degree and the appliance, which became embedded in a house wall, was wrecked. The incident was the Brigade's worst accident involving a fire appliance and was a major tragedy. Afterwards, the appliance bell was made into a memorial and kept at Moss Side for many years.

One of the Brigade's main priorities at this period was its rebuilding programme. Two thirds of the stations had been erected in the days of horse-drawn appliances and the living quarters were long out of date.

A new station was in course of construction at Blackley, on Rochdale Road. Due to the difficulties of

---

CITY OF MANCHESTER

PUBLIC NOTICE

The fire station at Ash Street, Harpurhey, will close at 9-0 a.m. on Thursday, 27th February, 1964. The area of the City previously protected by appliances based at that station will, thereafter, be protected by appliances from the new fire station situated at :-

ROCHDALE ROAD,
OPPOSITE KERR STREET,
BLACKLEY

To call the Fire Brigade in an emergency DIAL CENtral 2222 or DIAL 999. Alternatively, the Brigade may be called from any Police Station, or Police Box.

PHILIP B. DINGLE,
Town Clerk.

Town Hall,
Manchester, 2.
24th February, 1964.

---

designing the building, much of which would have to be below street level, the station did not become operational until 1964, a welcome replacement for the dilapidated Ash Street. It was one of the few MFB stations without a pole but the firemen soon became used to the idea of running *upstairs* when the bells sounded!

A number of interesting new ideas were incorporated into the station, including a deep-lift well for testing fire pumps. In accordance with the policy of unmanned watchrooms, full remote-control facilities were installed, which even allowed the appliance-room doors to be opened and closed from Headquarters. The most noteworthy feature, however, was an ultra-modern breathing-apparatus training complex. A sophisticated "maze" was provided, incorporating variable partitions and electronic floor pads, enabling the instructor to monitor the students' progress on a special console.

Three appliances were placed "on the run" at Blackley, including the last of the Leyland Firemaster pump escapes, and a new salvage tender to cover the north side of the city. The Brigade was rapidly modernising its fleet of special appliances as the various converted wartime vehicles became worn out.

The most interesting new appliance arrived in February 1964 and, with some justification, was described by the Brigade as "the first really new idea in firefighting in fifty years". The Simon "Snorkel" hydraulic platform featured a cage which could be raised to a height of 65ft giving the appliance a very great advantage over a turntable in that persons could be brought safely from a building without the need to climb down ladders. Firemen using the water monitor in the cage would have more room and versatility than with a turntable ladder.

Conditions for the firemen were improving. Domestic chores and the cleaning of station windows were handed over to civilians which gave the men more time to attend to their professional duties. In 1965 a controversial £45 per annum productivity bonus was agreed, in recognition of the men's willingness to provide cover for the emergency call-out scheme and to undertake extra duties such as juvenile training.

Meanwhile the City Council was occupied with the passage through Parliament of another local Act, part of which would effectively close a loophole in the licensing laws. It was known that a large number of establishments were operating in the City providing dancing and other entertainment but which, because they served no liquor, did not require a licence. These "Coffee Dance Clubs" along with bingo clubs and the like were regarded by the fire service as being as much at risk as licensed clubs, and under the Manchester Corporation Act of 1965 controls were introduced. It would now be necessary to register such premises with the Local Authority. The provision of adequate fire precautions would be a condition of such registration.

Blackley Fire Station.

Blackley Fire Station BA Training Control Panel.

The Simon 'Snorkel' 65 ft. hydraulic platform delivered 1964.

HMI Dann inspecting members of the AFS c1966.

Albion/Cocker pump (1966) seen on Fitzgeorge Street, Collyhurst.

1966 foam tender, built by Pyrene on an Albion chassis.

However, in all probability the most worrying area of fire risk in Manchester at this period was the ever-growing number of lodging houses and flats, principally in Moss Side and Whalley Range. The housing here consisted mainly of three-storey Victorian properties, many in a run-down condition, and some accommodating up to ten families. Cooking facilities and paraffin heaters could be found in almost every room. In one lodging house fire in Demesne Road, sixteen people were lucky to escape with their lives. Deputy Chief Officer Whiteside justifiably reported that the Brigade was "worried" about houses used as flats which had only one staircase. Although legislation existed requiring landlords to provide means of escape from such premises, many avoided their obligations by failing to register with the Local Authority. It profited the landlords not to register as the provision of adequate fire escapes could prove expensive. When such premises were located and requirement notices served for fire prevention work the landlords often gave tenants notice to quit and vacate top floors rather than undertake the alterations.

One answer was to be found in the Brigade applying a reasonable and very realistic approach to the problem. To require a full external fire escape staircase in such property would be counter-productive as the owners would simply evict their tenants. Instead an iron fire balcony would be provided, at second floor level, on a face of the building which offered good access for the fire brigade. Associated internal improvements would help ensure that persons using the balcony would be safe from fire and smoke while they waited. Experience had shown that appliances could reach most of these house fires in 3-4 minutes and the occupants could then be safely rescued from the balcony by firemen; indeed several rescues were ultimately made in this fashion from lodging house fires. Although not an ideal solution, the balconies saved many lives in situations where unscrupulous landlords would otherwise have provided nothing at all.

There was a sharp increase in lodging house fires in Moss Side during 1964 and 1965. Twenty-one people escaped from one house in Cecil Street; and thirteen persons survived a blaze in Meadow Street in which four others died. Despite an intense campaign during 1965 in which the Brigade carried out over 2,000 inspections and successfully prosecuted thirty-four landlords the problem, if anything seemed to be getting worse. The situation finally came to a head during the winter of 1965/66 when in one week fire claimed the lives of nine people (eight of them children) in Moss Side and Whalley Range.

A major new offensive was launched with the intention of stamping out the problem once and for all. The number of inspections was practically doubled and although the campaign did not completely eradicate the dilemma, the Brigade's high profile attempt to raise standards of such property did meet with success. In 1967 (the first full year of the campaign) fatalities were down by almost a half and injuries were cut by a third.

A number of interesting new developments were taking place in the Brigade's equipment. Plastic fire hose was introduced in 1966, along with the first compressed air breathing apparatus which would eventually replace the oxygen sets. Also in 1966 a new foam tender went into service at London Road and the Brigade undertook a series of trials to assess a new firefighting technique using bulk carbon dioxide. After successful tests and long negotiations an agreement was reached in 1968 with a local chemical firm for the supply of carbon dioxide in tankers directly to the fireground as required. This scheme, once it became operational, was shared by all the local brigades, though its actual use proved to be minimal. Another interesting development during the year was the invention by the Brigade Engineer, John Stevenson, of a device to ease the removal and replacement of fire appliance ladders. The new method, incorporating hydraulics to raise or lower the ladder whilst on its mounting became a standard feature of all Manchester machines.

Another "standard" in the MFB was that of unflinching pluckiness on the fireground. At an incident at a house in Ellenbrook Road, Woodhouse

Serious fire at a multi-occupied building, High Street, City, 15th July 1966..

A wheeled escape is trundled into position at a fire in Newton Street.

Park, a father was trapped upstairs overcome by smoke. Without wasting a second twenty-year-old fireman Peter Shalliker, raced up a builders ladder only to find out that due to the oxygen set on his back, he could not get through the window. Quickly discarding the bulky breathing apparatus, Shalliker climbed into the smoke-filled bedroom, despite cutting his arm and hand badly on the broken glass. Groping around in the hot, smoke-filled house he managed to find the unconscious man after searching four bedrooms. At this point, Leading Fireman, Robert Megram, managed to fight his way up through the house to help and, together, they were able to rescue the man who later recovered in hospital.

Afterwards Megram and three other firemen received commendations for their bravery, whilst Shalliker was awarded the BEM in March 1967. To cap this honour he was also elected as one of the "Men of the Year" and received his award at the Savoy Hotel in London.

Meanwhile the Brigade's Chief Fire Officer, Commander Hoare, was similarly becoming the centre of attention once more.

After 29 years service, most of it as Chief Officer, he was rightly regarded as one of the fire service's most colourful personalities and the events surrounding his retirement were entirely characteristic of the man.

As his 60th birthday loomed up in the summer of 1967, the Commander knew that, on reaching that age, it would be compulsory for him to retire from the service. Being still very much fit and well, and having in mind the recent retirement of Deputy Chief Officer Whiteside he applied for an extension of service. The Establishment Committee, however, flatly turned down the application. Their recommendation receiving support from the Council.

However, in between the Council's decision in early March and Hoare's birthday in July some frantic homework was done. It transpired that, in accordance with the terms of his transfer to Manchester, in 1948, the Commander retained certain rights from his days with the London Fire Brigade. Under these rules he was entitled to remain in post until he reached 30 years service and thus qualified for a two-thirds pension. This effectively

Senior officers 1968.

meant another year, even though he would then be 61.

The list of honours that Kenneth Newcome Hoare had earned are almost too numerous to mention, and include President of the Institution of Fire Engineers, Council member of the Chief Fire Officer's Association and Honorary Chief of the Manchester (New Hampshire) Fire Department. He held the Coronation Medal and the Queen's Fire Service Medal, served on the Home Office Committee on Fire Station design, and negotiated the reciprocal arrangements between the Institution of Fire Engineers and the Fire Services Central Examinations Board.

He was a great believer in the value of youth and enthusiasts' organisation and in 1964 he became the first ever president of the Fire Brigade Society, the now international fire enthusiasts' club when it was only one year old. The achievement of which he was personally most proud was when, as Chairman of the London Fire Brigade Sports Club, he, with Ronald Greene, founded the LFB Benevolent Fund. Out of this small beginning grew the Fire Services National Benevolent Fund of which the Commander was later Chairman, Vice-Chairman and President.

The enormous void created by the retirement of the city's second longest serving Chief was admirably filled by his Deputy, Harry Lomas, and with his promotion the Brigade enter its final phase. The new Chief appointed on 13th June 1968, had served all his career in Manchester, joining as a fireman in 1939 and being promoted Leading Fireman in the early days NFS. After a short break of four years serving with the Royal Marines in Burma and as an OCTU Staff Instructor, he returned to Manchester. Successive promotions saw him serving in various parts of the city and he soon earned the reputation of being a tough, no-nonsense operational officer of the Sloan type, rarely smiling and known to instil the fear of God into his subordinates.

Harry Lomas was a dedicated firefighter who always demanded the same high standards from his men. Totally fearless on the fireground, he had an uncanny affinity with, and a remarkable mastery over fire, coming into his own at major incidents where his calm, professional manner was an inspiration to all. The appearance of Mr. Lomas at a large fire was invariably followed by its rapid subdual. Quietly giving instructions and always making sure he was completely - and immaculately - rigged before taking charge, he was truly a "general" among fire officers. His lecture on "Command at Fires" was a regular item on the Fire Service College curriculum and there was surely no-one more qualified to give it.

Although there were no immediate and dramatic changes in the Brigade once Lomas had taken over, his high principles and standards were gradually infused into all personnel. Manchester firemen were, of course, extremely experienced and highly professional already, but under Lomas' leadership there was not one who did not firmly believe that he

Harry Lomas, Chief Officer 1968-1974.

London Road Fire Station, early 1970s.

Albion/Carmichael Pump, Blackley, 1971.

Fire at Robert Street, Strangeways, 17th May 1971.

Fire at Polygon Avenue, Ardwick, 8th September 1971.

Fire at Cheetham Street, Newton Heath, 27th July 1971.

Fire at Holland Street, Miles Platting, 5th June 1972.

Control Room Staff, 1974. *top row (left to right)*: L. Bonner, A. Mander, C. Howard, A. Heywood, C. Miles. *second row (left to right)*: M. McIlroy, G. Gaffney, E. Bentley, B. Jackson, V. Pomfret, G. Price, L. Cronley. *front row (left to right)*: H. Proctor, E. Pollitt, CFO Lomas, AGO Caulfield, G. Galloway, H. Bould.

Scenes at fire, Bank of England Mill,
Carruthers Street, Ancoats,
September 1986.

Thompson Street 1988. Pictured above is the Brigade's low-height Dodge G16C/Saxon/Simon SS263 hydraulic platform. Pictured below is the latest Dodge/Mountain water tender.

WELEPHANT AND THE SMOKE DETECTOR

WELEPHANT CLUB INC. REG. CHARITY No. 2008173

WHEN WELEPHANT WAS JUST AN ORDINARY ELEPHANT, HE OFTEN USED TO HAVE HIS FRIEND SPIKEY AROUND TO STAY THE NIGHT. ONE NIGHT, LONG AFTER WELEPHANT, SPIKEY AND WELEPHANT'S MUM...

...AND DAD HAD GONE TO SLEEP, A FIRE STARTED DOWNSTAIRS. IT WAS CAUSED BY WELEPHANT'S DAD LEAVING THE LAMP AND TELEVISION PLUGGED IN... SAM THE SMOKE DETECTOR, WHO IS ALWAYS AWAKE...

...WAS WATCHING. HE GOT ONE SNIFF OF THE SMOKE AND STARTED TO SOUND THE ALARM. MUM AND DAD WELEPHANT WERE AWAKENED BY THE BLEEP, BLEEP OF SAM'S ALARM... "GET THE CHILDREN", SAID...

...WELEPHANT'S MUM. A SLEEPY WELEPHANT AND SPIKEY WERE QUICKLY AWAKE AND ON THEIR WAY DOWNSTAIRS WITH MUM AND DAD. "STRAIGHT OUTSIDE" SAID WELEPHANT'S DAD, "DON'T OPEN THE LOUNGE...

...DOOR. ONCE OUTSIDE, DAD CALLED THE FIRE BRIGADE, WHILST MUM KEPT WELEPHANT AND SPIKEY OUT OF THE WAY. "A GOOD JOB YOU HAD A SMOKE DETECTOR FITTED" SAID THE FIRE CHIEF TO WELEPHANT'S DAD, "IT DID...

...A GOOD JOB, AND YOU DID THE RIGHT THING IN GETTING EVERYONE OUT AND CALLING THE FIRE BRIGADE, WELL DONE". THE FIRE CHIEF DIDN'T NOTICE THE YOUNG WELEPHANT GAZING ADMIRINGLY AT HIS FIRE HELMET... "PERHAPS ONE DAY" THOUGHT WELEPHANT "I'LL BE A FIRE CHIEF!"

WELEPHANT CLUB IS SPONSORED BY BEAVERFOAM – FIRE RETARDANT FOAM FOR INDUSTRY AND HOME.

GREATER MANCHESTER COUNTY FIRE SERVICE

was part of the most effective firefighting team there ever was.

The number of turnouts made during 1968 topped the 10,000 figure for the first time, but the incidence of large fires was down; in fact, the Brigade had not attended a 20-pump fire for nearly two years.

However, the first months of 1969 saw a run of serious and potentially catastrophic fires taxing the abilities of Lomas and his men to the full. The most unusual occurred in January and involved a crew of firemen - and their Chief Officer - walking a mile to the scene. The incident was in the 7 ft. diameter cable duct which links the two telephone exchanges of Dial House in Salford and Ardwick, Manchester, and passing through the "Guardian" underground telephone exchange. Some seventy Manchester and Salford firemen were eventually on the scene and the fire, somewhere beneath Salford, was extinguished by men in breathing apparatus who walked all the way from the entrance shaft with the indomitable Lomas by their side.

One of the main areas of progress at this period was in the appliance fleet. Great strides were being taken towards a standardised layout of lockers and equipment for instance. A great deal of research was also being done into pump design and methods of operation. The findings showed that the previous generation of appliances were not really giving the Brigade what it required. The large 900 gallons-per-minute pumps were seldom used to full capacity in a city like Manchester, where large numbers of appliances could be quickly mustered, and were also very demanding of manpower. Similarly the high-pressure hose-reels, which had been a feature of the fifties and early sixties, were found to be causing certain technical problems and were rarely used anyway.

Coupled with these findings the increased use of breathing apparatus at incidents (necessitated by the greater abundance of toxic materials, and facilitated by the changeover to simpler sets using compressed air) had shown the need for a hose line which was more easily manipulated by BA men. Experiments

Garage fire, Stretford Road, Hulme, 1969.

with small diameter (one-and-three-quarter-inch) hose lines had proved successful and this new technique, combined with a larger water tank, was found to be very versatile, giving the manoevrability of hose reels but with a correspondingly greater discharge of water.

Thus all new appliances would heave ready-coupled one-and-three-quarter-inch hose stowed in an instant fashion, smaller-capacity 500 gallons-per-minute pumps with low-pressure hose reels and 300-gallon tanks. Rearward-facing crew seats would give an additional safety feature, especially when breathing apparatus - now stowed inside the cab - was being donned en route.

This attitude of striving constantly towards increased efficiency paid dividends in a climate where ever greater demands were being made on the Brigade's resources. Exciting new redevelopment schemes in the City centre and in the inner residential areas meant that, in some instances, the whole concept of firefighting had to be rethought.

The planners' desire to create pedestrian-only high-rise complexes was bringing new problems of access for appliances and suitability of equipment for both firefighting and rescue purposes. Here the firemen, armed with portable firefighting "manpacks" and two-way radio, needed to approach the scene on foot and relied heavily on internal features such as fire lifts and rising mains. The Fire Prevention Department's involvement at drawing-board stage and the effectiveness of local legislation ensured the inclusion of not only these prime facilities but also automatic fire detection and such sophisticated features as air-pressurisation systems. These were designed to control the movement of smoke and thus provide safe working areas for firemen when many storeys above ground.

The late sixties and early seventies saw the service being involved in three important inquiries - and their subsequent reports - which would directly

Fire following a collision between a molasses tanker and a car, Mancunian Way, November 1969.

affect its future. The 1969 report of the Royal Commission on Local Government produced the first inkling of change in local authority boundaries and thus the shape of fire brigades to come. Under new proposals, the formation of metropolitan counties, with one unified fire brigade in each, was envisaged.

This proposed change still seemed a long way off and the findings of the Departmental Committee of Enquiry into the fire service, under the chairmanship of Sir Ronald Holroyd were more eagerly awaited. The report was published in May 1970 after some three years' detailed study into every aspect of fire service organisation and operation. The Report discouraged local plus-payments for firemen made without the agreement of the National Joint Council, as was the case in Manchester. This additional allowance had been the subject of more controversy during 1969/70 when a proposed increase to £78 was quashed pending an investigation.

A national pay claim was only resolved with the agreement of the employers to set up an independent enquiry with an evaluation of the fireman's role. This enquiry, chaired by Sir Charles Cunningham, produced the third report in two years and proposed radical changes in pay structure. With the implementation of the new pay rates in 1972, the Manchester excess was phased out along with the emergency call-out scheme itself.

The Manchester Fire Brigade's reputation for "economy" was something of a misnomer where operational efficiency was concerned and pre-determined attendancies of six - and even seven - appliances were quite common in the City prior to 1974. With the nature of Manchester's fire risk - dense housing, a highly congested central commercial area, high-rise complexes and all kinds of manufacturing and storage premises, many of which were in reoccupied Victorian mills or warehouses - such a policy of always erring on the right side made good sense. This was proved time and time again by the results obtained on the fireground through having a large number of men and appliances on the spot at

Wheeled escape in use at an attic fire, Stockport Road, Longsight, 1971.

the outset. Most of the special appliances were concentrated at the Headquarters station on London Road and with machines from here responding to almost half of the total calls, it was hardly surprising that the building, erected in 1906 was beginning to show its age.

In 1969 the Committee had agreed to look into the possibility of replacing London Road with two new fire stations: one a six-bay Headquarters station in the New Cross area, around Rochdale Road, and a smaller four-bay station near to Downing Street. In view of Holroyd's recommendation that recruit training be centralised no plans were made for the inclusion of a new Training School. In fact the scheme never materialised principally due to the impending local government reorganisation.

The so-called Greater Manchester area was made up, so far as fire brigades were concerned of two city, six county borough and part of two county brigades. Not surprisingly, mutual assistance was both necessary and frequently-practised. A number of Manchester appliances were rushed into the Lancashire County area on the occasion of a serious mill fire at Ashton-under-Lyne in October 1971, which resulted in the death of Fireman Norman Nolan from Manchester's Blackley Fire Station. The incident, somehow all the more tragic for taking place outside the City boundary, came as a tremendous shock to the Brigade and broke a record of thirty years in which no Manchester fireman had lost his life on the fireground.

Six months later, City crews were attending an over-the-border fire at the Oldham Battery Company in Denton, Lancashire, when a roof collapsed, trapping and seriously injuring Station Officer Wilfred McLaughlan. He suffered terrible burns in the incident and, after several weeks in hospital, finally succumbed to his injuries in June. Station Officer McLaughlan was on his last tour of duty prior to retirement when the accident happened and it is ironic that the fires which cost the lives of both Nolan and McLaughlan - and spoilt Manchester's unblemished post-war record - both occurred in the same station area of a neighbouring fire authority.

ERF/HCB-Angus/Simon 'Snorkel' 85 ft. hydraulic platform, 1972.

A new fire station built at Moss Side in 1972 was part of a major rejuvenation of one of the City's most deprived areas and easily the Brigade's worst trouble-spot for house fires. Massive redevelopment enabled the two local one-pump fire stations at Moss Lane East, Moss Side and Great Jackson Street, Hulme, to be combined into one new station. From the outset, the new station was conceived as being part of the community. Local residents were invited onto the station at the official opening and when a long-awaited 85 ft. hydraulic platform appliance was handed over at the station the following June, the locals were given the opportunity to test its abilities by being "rescued" from a neighbouring block of flats.

Appliances and men from several of the surrounding brigades were called in to assist with a particularly fierce blaze in January 1973. The fire, at Frederick J. Abbot's newsprint warehouse on Potato Wharf was one of the swiftest seen in Manchester in many years and caused the Brigade to be engaged at the scene for over a week. At about 4.30 pm on a Friday afternoon a foreman spotted smoke and flames at one end of the huge single-storey building and ran to his office to summon the Brigade. He barely had time to make the call before the fire spreading rapidly across the large rolls of print literally drove him from the building. The Brigade was severely hampered by limited access and the danger of collapse. The sheer intensity of the inferno raging inside prevented entry for five hours. Even then the danger was far from over, huge rolls of paper, weighing several hundredweights each, were stacked to roof height and after being ravaged by fire began to collapse, so that the men were continually at risk from being crushed by the burning reels.

The Abbot's fire set the pattern for major fires during 1973, the Brigade's last full year of operation, during which over 12,000 calls were dealt with. Two weeks after the Potato Wharf incident, ten pumps attended another serious warehouse fire, also in the Castlefield area, and at the end of the same week fire crews were astounded by the development of a fire at the Burgess Becker Primary School in Harpurhey. The school had been built to a standard prefabricated design known as C.L.A.S.P., which was used for schools, day centres

CFO Lomas with members of the First Aid Team c1972.

and residential homes all over the country. Unfortunately the dangers of its combustible construction and concealed voids were not fully appreciated until a number of serious fires occurred, notably at the Fairfield aged persons' home in Nottinghamshire at the end of 1974, in which eighteen people were killed. Had the Harpurhey fire not occurred during a half-term break the results could have been equally horrendous.

With only months left before local government reorganisation, planning for the new Brigade was by now well under way. The Greater Manchester Fire Service would take over 41 fire stations and about 2,000 personnel with Manchester being the largest of the wholly-absorbed constituent brigades.

With the changeover date approaching fast, senior officers were anxiously monitoring progress on the City's last new fire station. The £100,000 building being erected at West Gorton was the long-awaited replacement for Upton Street which had been opened in 1892, condemned in 1937 and *nearly* replaced in both 1939 and 1948. Because Upton Street was in the Everton Road slum clearance area, its closure had eventually been forced on the Brigade. The station was being upgraded to two pumps and an increase in Brigade establishment from 353 men to 368 had already been approved. A brand new appliance called the *Simonitor* - something of a cross between the hydraulic platform and a pump escape - had been delivered and was being fitted out at Headquarters in readiness for the new station.

Training of the drivers in the operation of the new machine would also have to take place before it could go into service.

With the April 1st deadline drawing near it was decided to officially open the station before it was finished. Accordingly, the Lord mayor Ald. Kenneth Collis, in what was the Brigade's last official ceremony, declared the building open on 26th March 1974, only five days before the appointed day and over a month prior to the station actually going operational.

It was also one of the last official duties for Chief Officer Harry Lomas who had been in command since 1968. Afterwards at a dinner held on the final weekend he was presented with an engraved silver salver by members of the Officers' Mess.

Several of those officers would be taking up senior appointments in the GMC Fire Service, but for Mr. Lomas the transition into the new Brigade would mark the beginning of a well-deserved retirement. In his final report to the Licensing and Fire Brigade Committee Mr. Lomas said he was "confident" that the MFB "will play an effective role in the forthcoming amalgamation", adding that "its record of service to the community of Manchester" was "of an extremely high order".

That record of service, stretching back two centuries, had been as consistent as it had been loyal and, in retrospect, each period of the Brigade's noble history owed something to the men who commanded it.

From Isaac Perrins, the gentle giant, who gave his life fighting one of the City's earliest-recorded major fires, and Charles Anthony who organised the first municipal fire establishment in England, to the celebrated Alfred Tozer who made it one of the foremost brigades in the country and finally Harry Lomas, who saw the Brigade pass with dignity and pride into a new era. These officers, together with all the men and women who served over 200 years, have shaped the history of that unique and renowned organisation which was the Manchester Fire Brigade.

50 ft. *Simonitor*, the last appliance to be delivered to the MFB.

Chapter Ten

"POSTSCRIPT" - THE GMC FIRE SERVICE

"Inside two years the Manchester Metropolitan Brigade will be a shining star. It will number among the best in the world."

P. H. DARBY
Chief Fire Officer
Greater Manchester Fire Service, 1974.

The task of welding together Manchester and the othe nine constituent authorities into one unified fire service fell to Mr. Peter H. Darby, who was appointed Chief Officer Designate before the end of 1973. Mr. Darby, then Chief of the Lancashire Fire Brigade, was to be known as County Fire Officer which, if a little unorthodox, did accentuate the new Brigade's wider horizons. As with the 1948 reorganisation, Mr. Darby commenced operations several months prior to the appointed day of 1st April 1974.

The Headquarters of the GMC Fire Service was set up at Bolton Road, Swinton, though initially these were to be purely administrative. 41 fire stations across the county were grouped into five divisions, each with a Headquarters in one of the larger towns. Manchester's London Road station became the Headquarters of "E" Division, which also included the city's three northernmost sub-stations and four former Lancashire and Cheshire stations in the new Metropolitan Borough of Tameside. The remaining three Manchester stations were attached to the Stockport ("D") Division and effectively lost any administrative link with their former Headquarters.

The main fire control room for the Brigade was based at Agecroft fire station in Pendlebury and dealt with the northern side of the county. London Road control room, now completely modernised with a new "VFA" remote control system, still remained active however and became responsible for handling all calls in the new "D" and "E" Divisions, comprising all of Manchester city as well as Stockport and Tameside.

The new Brigade got off to a busy start on 1st April 1974 and responded to 4,000 calls for assistance in its first three weeks of operation. At the end of three months, this figure had risen to 16,000 and the Authority continues to be one of the busiest in the country. Its annual turnout figure is usually around 50,000 calls.

The formation of GMC Fire Service brought several changes affecting the firefighting arrangements within Manchester. A new mobilising system relying on Parish boundaries, and apparently more suitable for the less urban areas on the fringes of the County, replaced the City's street index which had served so loyally since the 1950s. Other changes saw reductions in Manchester's generous predetermined attendance methods, and also a phased decline in the number of vehicles on the run at London Road. Appliance resources now had to be rationalised and their availability throughout the complete brigade considered. The fitting of radio telephones to *all* special appliances was a welcome development which would assist vehicle movements across a larger area.

On 1st May 1974 the new Manchester station at Feltham Street, West Gorton, became operational and the now-decrepit Upton Street premises finally closed down. At the end of the month the Brigade fought its first large fire when more than 100 firemen tackled a serious warehouse blaze in Lower Vickers Street, Miles Platting, Manchester. The crews, many wearing breathing apparatus, fought for five hours to contain the incident. By the end of 1974, GMC had answered nearly 38,000 calls for assistance.

The introduction of a new 48-hour working week for firemen in late 1974, less than a year after the Brigade's formation, led to an early shortage of manpower and an intensive recruiting campaign. The training school at London Road was kept busy and because of the large influx of new entrants, some trainees were passed to the Lancashire Fire Brigade Training Centre at Chorley, and a number of GMC instructors seconded there also.

One problem encountered early in the Brigade's life was the lack of standardisation across the county. Many stations worked different duty systems on changeover, though this particular problem disappeared with the adoption of the 48-hour week. Equipment and local operational procedures varied considerably however. Brigades such as Manchester had their own standard appliances with identical pumps and equipment which worked well before reorganisation, but with the frequent interchange of personnel under the new authority it

Fire at Baron's Warehouse, Rochdale Road, 1975; probably the last major fire attended by the 1964 Bedford 'Snorkel'.

was important that methods be standardised. Breathing apparatus, for instance, is one area where it is essential that men on different stations all use the same design of set. As for the vehicles themselves, increased mileage and the fact that replacement programmes had been interrupted by reorganisation meant that many appliances were now past their best. A fleet of over fifty standard new appliances was received in a two-year period and brought the desired uniformity. A new 77 ft. hydraulic platform delivered to London Road brought a welcome retirement for the station's ageing Bedford appliance, commissioned only in 1964, but by now worn out after a lifetime of fighting Manchester's biggest fires.

One of the most noticeable changes for operational personnel was the distances now travelled on assistance and relief duties at major incidents across the area. Thus crews from the fringes of the county often found themselves attending city centre warehouse blazes or Salford ship fires, whilst firemen from the inner cities have helped out at protracted peat moss or moorland incidents. In the past the smaller brigades were unable to enjoy the wide availability of relief crews which would give their men the necessary rest and recuperation at the latter stages of a large fire. The ease with which pumps can now be mobilised across the whole Brigade area gives a much fairer spread of work among the staff.

Such movements vastly increase the range of experience of personnel. Greater Manchester's 500 square mile area comprises a unique mixture of fire risks, including the congested city centre itself, major chemical plants, dense housing of all types, an international airport, one of the country's busiest and most intricate motorway networks, busy rail links, extensive moorlands, cotton mills and docks, although the latter have all but vanished now. All these have, in fourteen years of the Brigade's existence, brought serious problems at some time. Not surprisingly, Greater Manchester's 2,000 firemen are amongst the most professional in the country.

Basement fire, Nurseryneeds, Deansgate, June 1977.

Mr. Darby left the Brigade at the beginning of 1977 to take up an appointment as head of the London Fire Brigade, and was succeeded by Deputy County Fire Officer Mr. Ronald A. Bullers. Only weeks after his commencement, the Brigade attended a tragic fire which demonstrated the serious risk in city-centre multi-occupied premises. The incident occurred in China Lane, Piccadilly, Manchester, when a fire, starting in a basement cafe, spread smoke and fumes through the building. Seven women nightshift workers in a small factory on the top floor were unaware of the blaze until cut off by smoke. Despite a speedy attendance by the Brigade, they were unable to save the lives of the occupants.

Through the new Brigade, the name of Manchester is still synonymous with the highest standards of firefighting, training and fire prevention. Greater Manchester Fire Service, with its history of fire tragedy, is probably the most progressive and campaigning authority in fire prevention matters. In this respect, the GMC Fire Service continues the excellent pioneering tradition of the City Brigade. A series of catastrophic fires including the tragic Woolworth's inferno, the Ringway Airport disaster and a number of horrendous incidents in domestic property have led to the Brigade spearheading demands for improved safety in the field of upholstered furniture. The current changes in legislation affecting polyurethane foam fillings are a direct result of Greater Manchester's high profile campaigning, led by Assistant Chief Fire Officer Bob Graham, the county's senior fire prevention officer.

The nationally-known "Welephant" mascot, familiar to all children as the comical elephant in a fireman's uniform who *never* forgets his fire safety drill, was born in Greater Manchester. The character was dreamt up by 14-year-old Susan Buttner in 1979, as part of a local poster competition and its phenomenal success is now legendary. In Greater Manchester, *every* primary-school child is a member of the Welephant Club, and receives regular updates and fire safety advice from the Brigade.

Greater Manchester is also in the forefront of technical developments, especially in the field of control and mobilising. The Brigade commissioned the country's first wholly-computerised fire control room in new purpose-built premises adjoining the Swinton Headquarters. This space-age facility, which brought the closure of both Agecroft and London Road control rooms, is linked directly to all stations by high-speed printers, to transmit fire calls and other messages. The computer enables streets to be located and the nearest available resources are dispatched at the flick of a switch. Once on the road, the appliances are in constant touch with Control by means of the latest push-button radio equipment, which automatically updates the computer by standard coded transmissions. These also enable the Brigade's four busy radio channels to remain clear of routine messages for much of the time. The new control room complex, and Headquarters, was officially opened by HRH The Prince of Wales on 29th November 1979.

The present decade has seen the Brigade dealing with ever more frightening fire situations. Major civil disturbances in Manchester's Moss Side brought unprecedented problems for three nights in the summer of 1981, when rampaging mobs set fire to shops and other property in an area close to the district's fire station. Traditional firefighting techniques whereby fire crews rush straight to the scene of an incident - and are welcomed by the populous - had to be abandoned in favour of stand-off measures and the use of rendezvous points outside the danger zone. The situation was in some respects reminiscent of wartime mobilising procedures, but, thanks to the professionalism of all involved, was handled as smoothly as could be expected.

A series of frightening chemical incidents, of vast proportions, notably at the Chemstar reprocessing plant in Tameside and Flax Street in Salford, caused widespread public panic and concern whilst providing the Brigade with firefighting and mobilising problems of great magnitude. A major fire at the Anchor Chemical Co. in Clayton, Manchester in 1984, resulted in less overall devastation, but highlighted the risk of inner city areas where housing and heavy industry still lie so close together.

A major conurbation such as Manchester also has an extensive rail network and two major incidents outside the City at the end of 1984 revealed the potential hazards passing through the area daily. Both involved fuel-tanker trains - the first a fatal crash and fire occurring immediately beside the busy urban motorway at Salford. A fortnight later, a 1300-ton petrol train derailed and caught fire in the centre of the one and a half mile long Summit tunnel, outside Rochdale, some 300 ft. underground. To cope with both these fires, the Brigade had to liaise closely with neighbouring

above: Fire at Woolworth's, May 1979.
right: Rear elevation of Murray House, China Lane, 1977, in which seven lives were lost.

brigades especially at the Summit incident which occurred right on the authority's boundary with West Yorkshire.

Rochdale Fire Station became, in 1983, the home of Greater Manchester Fire Service Museum, one of a small number of official Brigade museums in this country. Here the visitor can see many relics of Manchester's (and other local brigade's) history at first hand, and see how the Greater Manchester region first became one of the most significant areas in the history of firefighting.

In Manchester, the most noticeable change, and one which most truly marks the end of the MFB era (if twelve years after reorganisation), has been the final closure of London Road Fire Station. Despite various proposals for the building in GMC's lifetime, including total refurbishment and a contraction of the amount of space occupied for fire service purposes, it was finally decided to replace the famous landmark with brand new premises. Deterioration of the fabric of the building pointed to higher and higher upkeep costs and it seemed the best course of action.

Centralisation had brought about removal of the Control room, workshops and stores, and large parts of the building now remained unused, particularly as the living quarters became vacated.

A new Divisional Headquarters fire station and Training School was opened at Thompson Street, Ancoats, in 1986 with an image suitable for the 1990's and beyond. Every modern facility was provided particularly in the Training Centre which is now one of the leading establishments in the country. The official opening of the extensive new complex by County Councillor Len Thomas, Chairman of the Fire Service Committee was in March 1986 and timed to precede the reorganisation deadline of 1st April when the GMC itself was phased out.

Today, London Road still stands forlorn, its future in the hands of private enterprise still uncertain, but Thompson Street is a shining beacon, the new focal point of Greater Manchester Fire and Civil Defence Authority's firefighting operations in Manchester.

MAJOR EVENTS

1615	First firefighting equipment in Manchester
1699	First fire engines purchased
1765	Manchester and Salford Police Act-powers to provide firemen and engines
1799	Appointment of Conductor (Isaac Perrins) and 21 men
1801, Jan. 27	23 killed in factory fire, Oxford Road
1810	Installation of stone water mains begun
1825	Fire station opened, Clarence Street
1826	Fire Engine Establishment formed
1843	Watch Committee took over fire brigade
1847, Aug. 11	Market Street fire
1850	Commencement of Longdendale high-pressure water supply
1860	First escape station (Piccadilly)
1863	First use of telegraph
1864	Reorganisation completed - 100% permanent men
1866	New Chief Fire Station, Jackson's Row
1870	First horses purchased
1871	First steam fire engine
1894	Opening of Thirlmere Water supply
1898	Brigade separated from Police
1899	First horse-drawn escape
1900	"Flying Squad" formed
1901	Gamewell fire alarm system installed, Docks
1904	First turntable ladder, Air-and-Light Engine, and fireboat *Firefly*
1906	New Headquarters fire station, London Road
1909, Feb. 8	Nine killed in lodging house fire, Grosvenor Street
1911	First motor fire engine; introduction of street fire alarm system
1911, Oct. 11	Fire, Anglo-American Oil Co., Trafford Wharf Road
1916, Feb. 29	Fire, SS *Spiraea*, Mode Wheel
1917	Last street escape stations closed
1917, June 13	Munitions explosion, Ashton-under-Lyne
1917, Oct. 2	Munitions explosion, Morecambe
1917, Nov. 10	Fifteen killed in fire, Delaunays Institution
1919	Last horses dispensed with
1920	Brigade re-amalgamated with Police
1921, Nov. 21	Celluloid film fire, Great Ducie Street
1924	First motor turntable ladder; fireboat *Firefly* handed over to Canal Co.
1930	First self-contained oxygen breathing apparatus
1931	First motor pump with tank and hosereel; first motor emergency tender
1934	First 100ft. all-steel turntable ladder
1936, Jul 8	Trafford Park timber fire
1938	Auxilliary Fire Service formed
1940, Dec. 22/23	Manchester Blitz
1941, June 2	Whit Sunday Blitz
1941, Aug. 18	National Fire Service formed
1942, Feb. 11	Sixteen killed in Deansgate Hotel fire
1948, Apr. 1	De-nationalisation of fire service; London Road Training School commenced
1950	First limousine fire appliance
1953	Dennis-Metz automatic fire appliance commissioned
1953, Aug. 15	Irk Valley Train Crash
1953, Aug. 21	Fire, Jewsbury & Brown, Ardwick Green
1953	Brigade Silver Band formed
1957, Mar. 14	Air crash, Shadow Moss Road — 22 killed
1957, Sep. 8	Fire, Paulden's Store
1958	Manchester Corporation Act
1958, Jan. 17	Fire, Belle Vue
1959	Leyland Firemaster appliance commissioned
1958, Feb. 10	Fires, Flatley's & Burton's
1959, Mar. 31	Street fire alarm system abandoned
1960, Oct. 18	Fire, Rochdale Canal Co., Dale Street
1963	Junior Firemen scheme commenced; conversion to remote control turnout completed
1963, Mar. 8	Fire, Major Street
1964	Simon "Snorkel" hydraulic platform commissioned
1970, May 15	77 rescued from club fire, Moss Side
1973, Jan 26	Fire, F. J. Abbott, Potato Wharf
1974, Apr. 1	Formation of Greater Manchester Fire Service

above: The MFB's first turntable ladder acquired by the Brigade in 1904. *left:* A preserved steamer takes to the road in 1981. A delight to passers-by, enthusiasts and rose-growers.

ROLL OF HONOUR

6. 1. 1801	ISSAC PERRINS
14. 10. 1829	THOMAS TAYLOR (ROYAL EXCHANGE)
26. 8. 1838	JAMES WATSON
22. 3. 1850	CHARLES McGARRY
24. 4. 1850	JAMES NAYLOR
22. 10. 1860	GEORGE DEARDEN
14. 6. 1861	JOHN HULMES
12. 6. 1866	HENRY CLARK
11. 1. 1867	FRANCIS KING
18. 1. 1876	JOHN BRIERLEY
6. 11. 1880	RICHARD DILLON
29. 3. 1881	JOHN CURLEY
8. 4. 1881	WILLIAM GRIFFITHS
25. 8. 1883	JOSEPH MARSH
30. 11. 1894	RICHARD SYKES
28. 1. 1908	GEORGE HENRY GRIFFITHS
4. 6. 1910	HENRY KINGSLEY
26. 3. 1913	HALDON HOLE
10. 7. 1914	SAMUEL CARRADUS
10. 7. 1914	CHARLES DAVIDSON
22. 4. 1916	JOHN FINNEY
19. 7. 1916	JOSEPH RICHMOND
4. 3. 1925	ALEXANDER CHARLES MITCHELL

WORLD WAR II

22—24. 12. 1940	GEORGE ALBERT
22—24. 12. 1940	WILLIAM HENRY ANDERTON
22—24. 12. 1940	ALBERT R. ASHLEY
22—24. 12. 1940	ERNEST BALME
22—24. 12. 1940	F. BOTHWELL
22—24. 12. 1940	KENNETH GEORGE FENTON
22—24. 12. 1940	ARTHUR HALL
22—24. 12. 1940	JOSEPH SCOLLIERS HOPWOOD
22—24. 12. 1940	THOMAS KILLEEN
22—24. 12. 1940	ALEXANDER PAUL
22—24. 12. 1940	C. PIMBLETT
22—24. 12. 1940	R. SKELTON
22—24. 12. 1940	CHARLES HENRY SMITH
22—24. 12. 1940	H. WALTER SMITH
22—24. 12. 1940	WILLIAM HECTOR VARAH
22—24. 12. 1940	H. E. SHAKESHAFT (NANTWICH)
22—24. 12. 1940	WALTER H. TAYLOR (CLITHEROE)
22—24. 12. 1940	THOMAS HUGHES (OLDHAM)
22—24. 12. 1940	JOSEPH HILTON (OLDHAM)
22—24. 12. 1940	BENJAMIN SCHOLFIELD (OLDHAM)
22—24. 12. 1940	HAROLD SHAWCROSS (OLDHAM)
22—24. 12. 1940	JAMES DUNKERLEY SPALDING (OLDHAM)
22—24. 12. 1940	RALPH BURROWS (KIRKBY-IN-ASHFIELD)
22—24. 12. 1940	ALAN RICHARD DAY (KIRKBY-IN-ASHFIELD)
22—24. 12. 1940	JOSEPH HENRY WRIGHT (KIRKBY-IN-ASHFIELD)
22—24. 12. 1940	A. M. HOLT (URMSTON)
7. 5. 1941	WILLIAM BAGNALL
7. 5. 1941	LESLIE JAMES DAGGETT
8. 12. 1942	GEORGE LUNN
9. 6. 1955	PETER GOODWIN
18. 11. 1963	JOHN BARNARD
18. 11. 1963	DAVID STREET
22. 10. 1971	NORMAN NOLAN
9. 6. 1972	WILFRED McLAUGHLAN

FIRE STATIONS

STATIONS	Open	Closed
Engine Houses:		
Old Church Yard	1699	(1808)
Mr. Croxton's (address unknown)	(1742)	(1746)
Mr. Touchet's, King Street	(1753)	(1764)
Tib Lane	(1767)	(1781)
Angel Yard, Market Place	1770	(1781)
	(1797)	(1797)
Deputy Kay's, Milngate	1770	(1781)
Josiah Birch's, High Street	1770	(1781)
St. John's Church	1770	(1781)
St. Mary's Church	1770	1784
Soap Manufactury, Long Millgate	(1781)	(1781)
Back of North Parade, St. Mary's	1784	(1800)
Bridgewater Arms, Garden Street	(1794)	(1808)
Facing Old Quay, St. John's	(1794)	(1797)
Infirmary, Piccadilly	(1794)	(1825)
Lawrence's Coaching House, Sounding Alley	(1794)	(1797)
Milk Street	(1794)	(1797)
	(1815)	(1820)
Simpson's Factory, Miller Street	(1794)	(1833)
Smith's Foundry, New Cross	(1794)	(1794)
Sun Fire Office, Hatters Lane	(1794)	(1797)
Swan — inn, Deansgate	(1794)	(1804)
Police Office, Back King Street	1800	(1813)
New Cannon Street	(1800)	(1800)
Turner Street	(1800)	(1800)
Union Street, Ancoats	(1800)	(1820)
Lamp Office	(1809)	(1811)
Fennel Street	(1811)	(1820)
Pine Street	(1811)	(1813)
Water Street	(1813)	(1825)
Collier's Yard, Duke Street	1820	(1825)
Police Station, Kirkby Street	(1829)	(1838)
Escape Stations:		
Infirmary, Piccadilly	1860	1910
Assize Courts, Strangeways	1863	1890
Police Station, Cavendish Street, Chorlton-on-Medlock	1863	1898
Police Station, Fairfield Street	1863	1865
Police Station, Fairfield Street	1887	1902
Police Station, Livesey Street, Miles Platting	1863	1872
Police Station, Park Place, Hulme	1863	(1863)
St. George's Church, Chester Road, Hulme	1871	1874
Ellesmere Street, Hulme	1874	1914
Ardwick Green	1875	1897
Police Station, Brooke Street, Bradford	1885	1903
Police Station, Monmouth Street, Rusholme	1885	1886
Town's Yard, Monmouth Street, Rusholme	1886	1895
Police Station, Willert Street, Collyhurst	1887	1904
Police Station, 11 Cheetham Place, Woodlands Road, Cheetham Hill	1887	1890
Police Station, Ashton Old Road, Openshaw	1890	1903
Police Station, Derby Street, Cheetham	1890	1904
Ducie Bridge	1890	1911
Town Hall, Stretford Road, Hulme	1890	1908
Upton Street, Chorlton-on-Medlock	1891	1892
Police Station, Clarendon Road, Crumpsall	1891	1917
Police Station, Oldham Road, Newton Heath	1891	1912
Upper Brook Street, Chorlton-on-Mediock	1891	1898
Public Institute, Stockport Road, Longsight	1892	1908
Gorton Lane/Clowes Street, West Gorton	1894	1904
Norman Road, Rusholme	1895	1912
Denmark Road, Moss Side	1898	1912
Lower Ormond Street, All Saints	1898	1914
Police Station, Belle Vue Street, West Gorton	1904	1917
Wilbraham Road, Nr. Lloyds Hotel, Chorlton	1907	1917
Police Station, Wilmslow Road, Withington	1907	1917
H. Q. Fire Stations:		
Police Yard, Clarence Street	1825	1866
Jackson's Row	1866	1908
Fairfield Street/London Road	1906	1986
Hose Cart Stations:		
Police Station, Albert Street	1863	1871
Police Station, Bridgewater Street, Deansgate	1863	1877
Police Station, Kirby Street	1863	1865
Town Hall, Stretford Road, Hulme	1863	1885
Police Station, Swan Street	1863	1872
Police Station, Cheetham Hill Road	1865	(188-)
Police Station, Fairfield Street	1865	1887
Police Station, Harpurhey	1865	1877
Police Station, Willert Street, Collyhurst	1877	1887
Police Station, 11 Cheetham Place, Woodlands Road, Cheetham Hill	(188-)	1887
Town's Yard, Monmouth Street, Rusholme (ex-RFB 1885)	1886	
Hand Pump Stations:		
Police Station, Grove Street, Strangeways	1863	(1890)
Police Station, Kirby Street	1865	1889
Police Station, Bridgewater Street, Deansgate	1877	(1883)
Police Station, Newton Street	(1884)	1898
Town Hall, Stretford Road, Hulme	1885	1890
Police Station, Canal Street, Ancoats	1889	1898
Police Station, Albert Street	(1890)	1898
Police Station, South Street, Longsight	1891	1898
Police Station, Lowe Street, Newton Heath	1892	1898
Police Station, Belle Vue Street, West Gorton	1892	1898
Fire Stations:		
Town's Yard, Pollard Street	1843	1865
Police Station, Cheetham Hill Road	1863	1865
Boond Street, (Pollard Street)	1865	1938
Police Station, Park Place, Hulme	(1866)	1926
Goulden Street, New Cross	1872	1916
Trees Street/Crescent Road, Crumpsall (ex-CFB 1890)	1891	
Upton Street, Chorlton-on-Medlock	1892	1974
New Street, Miles Platting	1892	1967
Ash Street, Harpurhey	1892	1964
Mill Street, Bradford	1903	1967
Moss Lane East, Moss Side (ex-MSFB 1904)		1972
Gt. Jackson Street, Hulme	1928	1972
Altrincham Road, Sharston	1934	(1940)
Wilmslow Road, Withington	1938	
Sharston Hall, Altrincham Road, Sharston	(1941)	1957
Brownley Road, Wythenshawe	1957	
Rochdale Road, Blackley	1964	
Briscoe Lane, Phillips Park	1967	
Denhill Road, Moss Side	1972	
Feltham Street, West Gorton (Birch Street)	1974	
Hose Stations:		
Police Station, Cheetham Hill Road	1863	1865
Police Station, Harpurhey	1863	1865
Hand Pump Boxes:		
Brighton Grove, Rusholme	1892	1895
Cabman's Shelter, Fennel Street	1892	(1896)
Cabman's Shelter, St. Ann's Sq.	1892	(1896)
Cheetham Hill Road/Middleton Road, Cheetham Hill	1892	(1896)
Collyhurst Road/Rochdale Road, Collyhurst	1892	(1896)
Eye Hospital, Oxford Road, Chorlton-on-Medlock	1892	(1896)
Health Dept., Oldham Road	1892	(1896)
Liverpool Road	1892	(1896)
Oxford Street, Nr. Oxford Road — inn	1892	(1896)
Southern Hospital, Clifford Street, Chorlton-on-Mediock	1892	(1896)
Upper Brook Street, Victoria Park	1892	(1896)
Women's Home, Embden Street, Hulme	1892	(1896)
Fireboat Station:		
Docks, Trafford Park, Salford	1902	1924
Garages:		
Railway Arch, Bennett Street, West Gorton	1951	1968
No. 2 Arch, Store Street	1962	1970
Darcy Street, Moss Side (AFS)	1958	1969
Divisional H. Q. Station (GMCFS):		
Thompson Street, Ancoats	1986	

CHIEF OFFICERS 1799—1974

Isaac Perrins	Conductor	1799—1801
Thomas Knight	Conductor	1801—1812
William Vickers	Conductor	1812—1820
Phineas Sykes	Conductor	1820—1822
Richard Downing	Conductor	1822—1825
Capt. Charles Anthony R.N.	Superintendent	1826—1827
Thomas Gallimore	Temp. Superintendent	1827—1828
William Rose	Superintendent	1828—1846
Thomas Rose	Superintendent	1846—1862
Alfred Tozer	Superintendent	1862—1892
John Lacey Savage	Superintendent	1892—1899
George William Parker	Chief Officer	1899—1903
Frederic William Baylis	Chief Officer	1904—1916
Arthur Ready Corlett, OBE, KPFSM, MIFireE	Chief Officer; Chief Supt.	1916—1931
Daniel Devine Sloan KPFSM, MIFireE	Chief Officer; Chief Superintendent	1931—1936
David Drummond, MIFireE	Chief Officer	1936—1941
Francis Dann, OBE, LIFireE	Fire Force Commdr. (NFS)	1941—1948
Lt. Cmmdr. Kenneth Newcome Hoare, RN, (Ret'd), QFSM, FIFireE	Chief Fire Officer	1948—1968
Harry Lomas, CBE, QFSM, O. St. J., FIFIreE	Chief Fire Officer	1968—1974

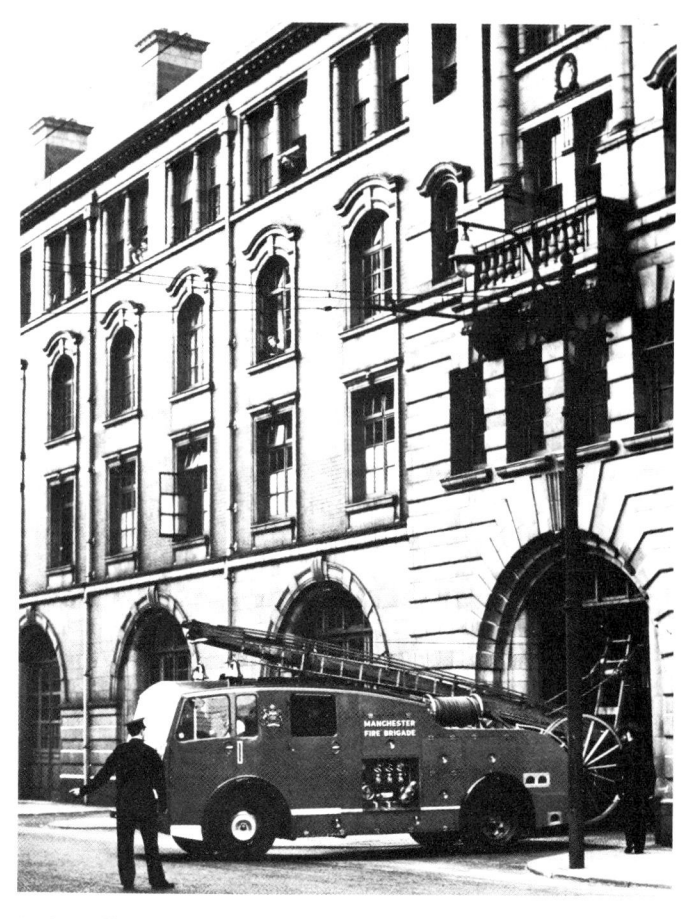

below: Escape Station, Norman Road, Fallowfield.